Publisher:
John Betancourt

Editor:
Marvin Kaye

Managing Editor:
George H. Scithers

Typesetting & Design:
Owlswick Press

Distribution Manager:
Warren Lapine

Contributing Editors:
Craig Shaw Gardner
Darrell Schweitzer

Copyright © 2005
by Wildside Press, LLC.
All rights reserved.

H.P. Lovecraft's Magazine of Horror™ is published four times a year by Wildside Press LLC, P.O. Box 301, Holicong PA 18928–0301.

Postmaster & others: send change of address and other subscription matters to DNA Publications, attn: *HPL Magazine*, P. O. Box 2988, Radford VA 24143. Single copies: $7.95 (magazine edition) or $19.95 (book paper edition), postage paid in the U.S.A. Add $2.00 per copy for shipping elsewhere. Subscriptions: four issues for $19.95 in the U.S.A. and its possessions, $29.95 in Canada, and $39.95 elsewhere. All payments must be in U.S. funds and drawn on a U.S. financial institution. If you wish to use PayPal to pay for your subscription, email your payment to: <wildside@sff.net>.

The publisher may be contacted at:

Wildside Press
Attn: *HPL Magazine*
P.O. Box 301
Holicong PA 18928–0301
www.wildsidepress.com

Writers and artists: query <HPL_Magazine@yahoo.com> prior to submitting any materials. We invite letters of comment, and we assume all letters received are intended for publication (unless marked "Do Not Publish") and become the property of Wildside Press.

BE HEARD!
Tell us what you think. Visit the official *H.P. Lovecraft's Magazine of Horror* message board at:

www.wildsidepress.com

H.P. LOVECRAFT'S MAGAZINE OF HORROR

Vol. 1 No. 2   **ISSN: 1552-8642**

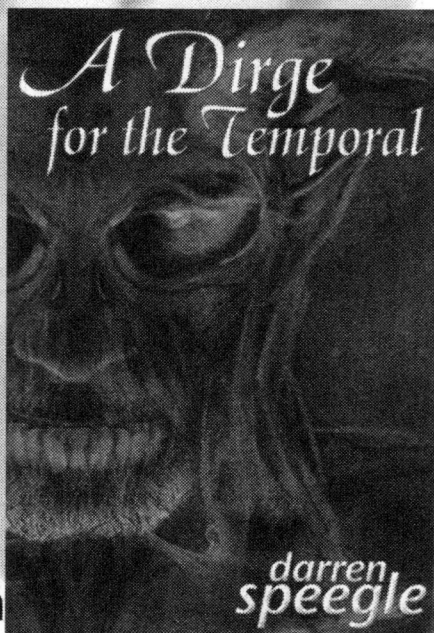

THE OUTSIDER'S DESK

I'm tempted to call this editorial "Growing Pains." It's been a while since our first appearance, and while we did publish an interim issue #1.5 (available only to subscribers), we seem to have started off as an annual, not a quarterly periodical. Two successive changes in distributorship accounted for our elongated timetable, but our publisher assures me that with this issue, *H. P. Lovecraft's Magazine of Horror* truly becomes a quarterly.

When we first appeared, we received many excellent submissions of new stories and articles and bought enough of them to fill several issues. The delay, therefore, has been especially frustrating because of the number of times I've had to tell querying writers, "Not now, but try us again in X number of months." Only X became Y, and Y had to be reedited to Z. So those of you who wish to submit new fiction, nonfiction, poetry, etc. — a good time to be in touch should be soon after our third issue appears. At that time, e-submissions may be sent to me in care of the publisher, <HPLmag@wildsidepress.com>.

I have been asked several times to provide submissions guidelines, but am reluctant to declare dictums. The scope of *HPL's* encompasses a very broad interpretation of fantasy, and especially horror. Gore has its place, but it must be uncommonly well done and essential to the plot to appear in this magazine.

The chief concern in each issue is to balance between contemporary fantasy-horror-terror, and echoes of Lovecraft. Our titular master will always be an important part of the mix, but never the only colour (out of space?) in these pages.

As an editor and as a genre book collector, I find it important to offer in each anthology — read: magazine — a combination of new fiction and little-known work by famous writers. I am particularly pleased with this issue for both reasons.

HPL's #2 gets off to a good Lovecrafty start with Greg Lamberson's report on Arkham-influenced films, John Glasby's eerie return to HPL's baleful seacoast town of Innsmouth, and Marc Bilgrey's nefarious doings at Montauk on the tip of Long Island. New stories include a highly original confectionary nightmare by Joel McRennary (a holdover crowded out of issue # 1), a deeply moving fantasy (one of her favorites) by Tanith Lee, as well as tales by Chris Bunch and R. J. Lewis.

Richard Matheson is especially featured this issue. There can be no argument, and Stephen King himself has said it: Matheson is the greatest living American horror writer. I think his masterpiece, *Hell House*, may be the best haunted house novel ever written, but one also cannot slight *I Am Legend*, *The Incredible Shrinking Man*, *A Stir of Echoes*, or his long series of stories, especially "Nightmare at 20,000 Feet." Thanks to Mike McCarty for interviewing the Grand Master, and for preparing a fascinating filmography as well.

When I asked Mr. Matheson whether he might send us a new story, I learned he is no longer writing short fiction — but he asked my old friend William F. Nolan to get in touch. To my awed delight, I learned that — though Bill had published a collection of Matheson's hitherto-unpublished stories a few years ago — a couple had not been included. "He Wanted to Live," which I am told has autobiographical undertones, is one of these tales. Thanks to Bill Nolan, it appears in these pages for the first time.

CLASSIC PULP FICTION FROM WILDSIDE PRESS!

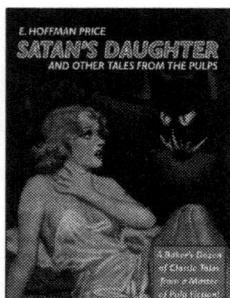

Satan's Daughter and Other Tales from the Pulps
by E. Hoffman Price. Intro by Darrell Schweitzer

A baker's dozen of classic pulp stories, by a master of the genre! *Satan's Daughter and Other Tales from the Pulps* includes such rare gems as the title story, "Scourge of the Silver Dragon," "Revolt of the Damned," "Pit of Madness," "The Walking Dead," "Drink or Draw," and many more. A delightful selection, ranging from fantasy to horror to action-mystery, all sprinkled with a dash of erotica.

Out of the Wreck and Other Nautical Tales
by Captain A. E. Dingle

Captain A.E. Dingle published sea stories in the pulp magazines for decades, and the volume, quality and variety of his tales is nothing short of astonishing. This collection assembles eight of his finest, from the Sherlock Holmes pastiche "Watson!" to the short novel "The Coolie Ship," from the misadventures of "Skimps, Ship's Boy" to the lives of "Hard-Shell Clammers" -- nautical stories told by a master craftsman!

The Mysterious Wu Fang: Case of the Suicide Tomb
by Robert J. Hogan

The ancient tomb had been sealed for a thousand years; its discovery was an archaeological find. But few guessed its horrible secret, or knew that an Oriental super-villain, the fiendish Wu Fang, wished to enter its portals to capture the death germs buried there -- deadly germs of a rare plague of madness which he meant to use to control the world! From the December, 1935 issue of *The Mysterious Wu Fang* magazine, presented with its original cover and interior art.

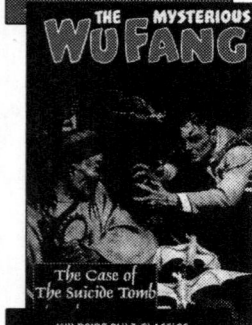

Operator #5: Blood Reign of the Dictator
by Curtis Steele

Operator #5 appeared in more than 48 novels in the pulp magazine bearing his name. From April 1934 to November 1939, Jimmy Christopher fought villains from inside the United States and invaders from without. With World War II looming on the horizon, the Operator #5 books became a reflection of the times -- none more so than when a fascist dictator appears to take over the U.S. government! *Blood Reign of the Dictator* is a classic entry in the series.

Secret Agent "X": The Legions of the Living Dead
by Brant House

From the September, 1935 issue of *Secret Agent X* comes this sensational novel: "From nowhere hurtled that black death car. And from nowhere came its grisly occupants. They were not of the earth, for their human flesh was immune to bullets. They were not of the grave, for they manned the wheel and a blasting machine gun- Secret Agent "X" made a desperate maneuver to block their invasion of the land of the living. And in that weird terror trap, he came face to face with a man he knew had died five years ago!"

Another "first" in this issue is the posthumous tale by Jean Paiva, who died of cancer a few days after completing her second fantasy novel, *The Last Gamble*. Thanks to her agent Donald Maass for providing me with the files of her eleven unpublished short stories, two others of which have appeared in my anthologies. This is the second to appear in *H. P. Lovecraft's Magazine of Horror*.

Ray Russell's poignant fantasy is a semi-first. Though a revised version of it appeared in his Hollywood novel, *The Colony*, Ray preferred it in its original form and hoped I might be able to use it in one of my anthologies. Though the character name has been changed, this is Ray's lament for his friend, the late great fantasist Charles Beaumont.

AND THINGS TO COME . . .

The featured author of the third issue of *H. P. Lovecraft's Magazine of Horror* will be the renowned British fantasist Brian Lumley. In addition to an interview with him by Darrell Schweitzer, two new stories will appear, one of them with distinctly Lovecrafty overtones.

Also look for a new adventure of the great, albeit put-upon sorcerer Johannes Cabal, whose first adventure appeared in *HPL's* #1; an amusing riff on a school similar to Harry Potter's Hogwarts — up to a point! — and, space permitting, fantasy tales by Mike Allen, Ron Goulart, Darrell Schweitzer, and Chelsea Quinn Yarbro.

—Marvin Kaye

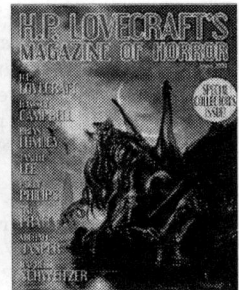

Horror for Mr. Grumpy

by Craig Shaw Gardner

As I mentioned in my very first column in these parts, I love short stories. Especially horror short stories. Back in the seventies, those old *Shadows* anthologies were my favorite beach reading. There's just something about reading really dark stories on really sunny days . . .

So it's no surprise that I'm looking at more of that short stuff. But riddle me this, reader: When is an anthology of great stories not a great anthology? It happens here when the editor succeeds a bit too well.

I'm talking about **The Dark,** the most recent anthology from the award-winning editor Ellen Datlow. The stories here are about as well-written as you can get, penned by some of the top names in the field. And each story I read gave me the same eerie feeling, more a delicate thrill than a scare.

And that's the problem.

I read *The Dark* a few months back, just as a slight hiccup in the *H.P. Lovecraft's* production schedule delayed the publication of the magazine for a bit. Well, fair enough, methinks, since I can still produce a review in time for the book's paperback edition. But then, when I went back to reconsider the book, I found I had trouble remembering the individual stories. As I browsed through them again, I recalled liking a number of them when I first read them, especially nice pieces from Gahan Wilson and Charles Grant. The Kelly Link story, "The Hortlak," has a particularly strange and wonderful ending. There's not a really bad story in the book — the worst I can say is that the Lucius Shepherd piece, "Limbo," would have been better at half its current length. But I also remembered how I started to feel slightly dissat-

isfied as I continued through the book the first time.

These stories are all very much of a piece. They are not simply ghost stories, they are all a certain type of ghost story. It's the "eerie otherness" tale — the sort of thing calculated to send a gentle chill down your spine — and certainly a legitimate branch of horror fiction, reaching back to the day when Victorian ladies wrote this sort of tale. But a certain sameness creeps in when eeriness is all you get. As I read one nicely turned story after another, I kept hoping for one, good old-fashioned scare. Nope. Just more refined eeriness. As I looked back on the collection, everything in the book blends, washes, recedes. In the end most of these stories just passed on by, without leaving much of an impression.

Obviously, Datlow had a vision for these stories. It's just not my vision. As I write this, the collection has already won a Horror Guild award and is nominated for a Stoker. So maybe I'm just being grumpy here. But I think the reader would be better served by reading the stories in *The Dark* over time, with other stories in between.

Editor Robert M. Price has revived an old pulp magazine in book form with **Strange Tales of Mystery and Terror.** The spine proclaims this to be volume 4, number 1. And these stories have a bit of the pulp and horror history in them. (One is a "King in Yellow" story, and another mentions Hyperborea.) The stories are competently written, by and large, though they don't feature the nuances found in *The Dark.* The best tale in the book is "King Father Stone" by Darrell Schweitzer, a fable written in the manner of Lord Dunsany which has a nice

IF YOU LIKE YOUR FICTION HOT ...

Harp, Pipe, and Symphony, by Paul Di Filippo

$27.95 (500-copy HC; ISBN: 1-930997-80-9); $45.00 (100-copy signed HC with bonus chapbook)

In this, Di Filippo's first fantasy novel ever, Thomas the Rhymer confronts humans and faery and monsters, in a quest through lands known and unknown ... but can he survive the machinations of the Faery Queen?

He Do the Time Police in Different Voices, by David Langford

$16.95 (trade pb; ISBN: 1-59224-058-5); $29.99 (hardcover; ISBN: 1-59224-057-7)

A collection of Langford parodies and pastiches incorporating the whole of The Dragonhiker's Guide to Battlefield Covenant at Dune's Edge: Odyssey Two (1988, long out of print) plus some 40,000 words of additional material.

The Rose of Heaven, by Michael Hemmingson

$17.95 (trade paperback; ISBN: 1-930997-55-8);$29.95 (hardcover; ISBN:1-930997-54-X)

The year is 1910. In a devout Catholic community in California, a young girl, Rosina, exhibits a tendency for miracles — the ability to heal and bring the dead back to life. Some worship and adore her. Others fear and wish to kill her. And others, like a priest sent by the Vatican and a few opportunistic government operatives, harbor dreadful designs on her phenomenal powers...

The Nature of Balance, by Tim Lebbon

$29.95 (hardcover; ISBN: 1-89481-516-5)

One morning the world does not wake up. Millions lie dead in their beds, victims of their own dreams of falling. There are survivors ... but the world they emerge into is changing rapidly. Humanity is no longer the dominant species. Now, Nature has the upper hand.

Pain Machine, by Marcy Italiano

$15.00 (trade paperback, ISBN: 1-59224-104-2)

Dr. Veronica Laka may seem like a harmless old lady, but with her partner Dr. Mark Ivy, the pain machine was born, a device that can transfer pain from one person to another. First, they have to figure out how to measure pain on levels. Then, they have to find a human volunteer, a person who feels the pain, and a doctor to accept it by going "under the wires."

---

twist of its own. The stories here seem pretty evenly divided between horrible things in ancient kingdoms and terrible things happening to the guy next door. A couple of the stories are a bit predictable in that old-school-horror sort of way. I guessed the ending of Stanley Sargent's "Famine Wood," which is something of a tall tale, a few paragraphs in. There's a little "eerie otherness" here, too, but this is more your meat-and-potatoes horror. Most importantly, it's an entertaining mix. *Strange Tales* is a good place to go if you want some old fashioned scares. I hope there's a Volume 4, Number 2.

Want something even more varied? Try **Borderlands 5,** edited and published by the husband-and-wife team of Tom and Elizabeth Monteleone. Heck, they don't even call this a horror anthology — according to a blurb on the cover, this is "an anthology of imaginative fiction." But terror and strangeness lurk on every single page. These stories work the borders between horror, modern fantasy, and magic realism, giving the *Borderlands* series a unique mix. As the cover copy says, "It is the intention of the editors to publish new, original short fiction which pushes the limits of what's being done in darkly imaginative fiction. Writers published in Borderlands will be part of the expedition to open the gates to new literary territory, and will help scorch a path though the jagged landscape of the imagination unbound . . . and all those other neat metaphors."

Scary and quirky; that's what that paragraph says to me. And true to the cover copy, there's all sorts of odd stuff here. The book begins with a Gary Braunbeck story about a guy whose face has very special powers, followed by a John Platt story about a man who wakes up every morning wearing a different person's hands, which is followed in turn by a well-told but much more traditional ghost tale by Holly Newstein, then next up is a Kafkaesque "report" from Adam Corbin Fusco in which people are being dispassionately murdered by researchers in comic costumes. Well, you get the drill. In these stories, anything can happen.

The current *Borderlands* collection is a big book, with big names like Stephen King and Whitley Strieber sharing space with authors at the beginning of their careers. Not all the stories are equally successful, but the tones and ideas held within always kept me completely entertained. My favorite story in the book is

"The Planting" by Bentley Little. The editors have stuck it midway through the book, and it seems like the perfect Borderlands story, where half the action exists in the real world, while the other half of it takes place somewhere else entirely. It concerns a man who steals an attractive woman's underwear, plants them in the ground, and urinates on them to get them to grow — something. In the meantime, the protagonist's real-life job as a firefighter intrudes in a realistic sequence where his company is called on to extinguish a blaze at a summer camp in the woods. But the burned camp reveals a formerly hidden, older cabin beyond the underbrush, a camp that appears to be the home of what one of the characters calls "God" — not "a god," we're working with a capital G here. But God resembles nothing in any religion I've ever heard of, and seems to get the protagonist and his compatriots to do unspeakable things, only hinted at, never explained. Of course, the results of the protagonist's planting show up in the mix, too. And somehow, by the devastating final line, it all makes a sort of illogical "sense."

The story manages to be irreverent, scary and funny all at the same time. It shows the possibilities inherent in horror, and imaginative fiction, that are all too seldom realized. Unlike the polished stories of *The Dark,* or the slightly retro but also slightly safe amusements of *Strange Tales, Borderlands* gives us all sorts of odd angles and shapes that might be a bit beyond description. The collection shows us that there is still something new — and surprising — in the fantastic. If you're looking for the possibilities inherent in horror, and aren't afraid of a few twisted tales along the way, you should give this collection a try.

Other short forms have crossed my desk in the past couple months, including a pair of interesting illustrated narratives. I'm talking comic books here.

Kwaidan is a graphic novel translated from the Japanese, and according to the notes, the title itself translates as "ghost story." You may already be familiar with the wonderful Kobayashi film of the same name (available on DVD) which collects five ghost stories of medieval Japan in a very colorful fashion, or of the original stories which inspired the film, written by Lafcadio Hearn, an Irishman who relocated in Japan and produced a number of books of spooky tales. If you liked either of these, you'll

like the new *Kwaidan* as well (and if you haven't seen the film or read the original stories, I recommend both of them highly.)

The graphic novel is an original tale, inspired by those earlier works but quite captivating in its own right. The art stands comparison with the high standards of European historical comics, and is reproduced in absolutely glorious color. The story concerns a girl born without a face, the blind monk who loves her, a cursed lake, and all sorts of evil spirits — including some particularly nasty children. I highly recommend it. The book comes from Dark Horse, a publisher that seems to have a liking for terror tales. You may have heard of another one of their characters, a fellow named Hellboy.

Recently, Dark Horse took over the publication of another horror-influenced series, the decidedly quirky *The Goon,* and they have recently issued three volumes of Goon stories in trade paperback. I'd recommend you start with the earliest Goon stories, collected in **The Goon, Rough Stuff.**

Powell's art takes its cue from the classic EC comics, with a little bit of Will Eisner's *Spirit* and the bizarre creations of Basil Wolverton thrown in. The story seems to take place sometime in the "past" from the look of the clothes and cars, only the Goon's hometown seems to be totally overrun by zombies. Not to mention unspeakable monsters, some of whom are working for the zombies. Thank goodness the Goon has two good fists that can smash just about anything! It's an odd mix of horror and humor that's quite cheerfully demented and equally entertaining. And *Rough Stuff* also

includes a number of pages where Powell shows us the evolution of the Goon, and his artistic style.

But I've saved one of the best, short things for last. I'm talking about a short novel by the editor of this very magazine, Marvin Kaye's **The Last Christmas of Ebenezer Scrooge.** In this gentle ghost story, Kaye manages to channel the spirit and style of Charles Dickens to give us the story of what happened to Scrooge, and Marley's ghost, after *A Christmas Carol.* It's a very involving and ultimately uplifting story, and a fine successor to Dickens's own Christmas tales. You could do far worse than settling down with your family this holiday season and reading this book aloud — it's that good — to revive that Dickens holiday tradition. Oh, and it has some good scary parts, too.

Good, short stuff is all around us. And that doesn't make me grumpy at all.

The Dark, edited by Ellen Datlow, TOR, hardcover, $25.95.

Strange Tales of Mystery and Terror, edited by Robert M. Price, Wildside Press, trade paperback, $12.50.

Borderlands 5, edited by Elisabeth E. Monteleone and Thomas F. Monteleone, Borderlands Press, $35.00.

Kwaidan, story and art by Jung and Yee-Yun, translated by Helge Dascher, Dark Horse Books, $14.95.

The Goon: Rough Stuff, story and art by Eric Powell, Dark Horse Books, $12.95

The Last Christmas of Ebenezer Scrooge by Marvin Kaye, Wildside Press, $15.95.

ARKHAM FILM VAULT

Lovecraft's Bad Book

by Gregory Lamberson

In his "Cthulhu Mythos," H.P. Lovecraft created *The Necronomicon*, a fictional book of the occult that appeared in several of his stories. Lovecraft introduced Abdul Alhazred, the "mad Arab," in his 1921 story "The Nameless City," and *The Necronomicon* in his 1922 tale "The Hound." He married the two in his 1926 classic, "The Call of Cthulhu," in which he revealed that Abdul Alhazred, an opium and hashish user, had written *Al Azif,* as the book is supposedly known in Arabic. The author's fictional 1927 treatise, "The History and Chronology of the Necronomicon," led many readers to believe that the tome was genuine. The evil book resurfaced in a prominent role in the 1928 story, "The Dunwich Horror," Lovecraft's most widely read work. In 1963, nearly three decades after Lovecraft's death from cancer, Hollywood first introduced filmgoers to his creation; since then, *The Necronomicon* has become a staple of Lovecraftian cinema.

Following the success of his Edgar Allan Poe film adaptations for American International Pictures, director-producer Roger Corman turned his attention to Lovecraft's short novel, "The Case of Charles Dexter Ward." Charles Beaumont, a fantasist who wrote twenty-one teleplays for Rod Serling's *The Twilight Zone,* crafted the screenplay. Judging by the film, *The Haunted Palace* (1963), Beaumont's admiration for Lovecraft did not extend to the novel he adapted. While *The Necronomicon* does make its first cinematic appearance, and the story takes place in Arkham, and Cthulhu and Yog-Sothoth are mentioned, the film bears little resemblance to Lovecraft's tale of alchemic possession.

Vincent Price, fresh from Corman's Poe pictures, stars as sorcerer Joseph Corwin and as his descendant, Charles Dexter Ward. In the opening, Corwin is about to sacrifice a shackled young woman to an unseen creature lurking in a pit in the titular palace when torch-wielding villagers intrude and burn him at a stake. Stuart Gordon echoed the staging of the aborted sacrifice in his 1992 Lovecraft adaptation, *Dagon.* The scene in which Corwin, burning, curses the villagers and their descendants, was copied from the prologue of John Llewellyn Moxey's atmospheric black and white chiller, *Horror Hotel* (1963). Possessed by his ancestor, Ward renews ancient experiments and mistreats his wife (Debra Paget). In typical A.I.P. fashion, a raging inferno consumes the palace at the end.

Corman's cast also featured veterans Lon Chaney, Jr., and Elisha Cook. He treated the material with respect and a great deal of visual flair: dense fog swirls, painted backdrops, and gothic sets lit with style. This remains the most beautifully filmed Lovecraft adaptation. In the film's most terrifying sequence, Price and Paget go for a late night stroll through the town of Arkham and find themselves surrounded by genetic mutants that foreshadow the denizens of Innsmouth in *Dagon.*

A.I.P. founders James H. Nicholson and Samuel Arkoff must not have shared Corman's enthusiasm for Lovecraft; although they gave the author screen credit, they promoted the film as "Edgar Allan Poe's *The Haunted Palace,*" deriving the title from a line in Poe's "The Fall of the House of Usher." Since Corman had directed Price in the film version of *Usher,* the decision made sense from a marketing standpoint. A similar fate befell Michael Reeves' beautiful 1969 Price vehicle, *Matthew Hopkins: Witchfinder General,* which was released as *The Conqueror Worm* to capitalize on a Poe poem, which the producers had Price recite at the film's start.

The Necronomicon did not appear in the next Lovecraft film, *Die, Monster, Die!* (1965). This horrible adaptation of the author's favorite story, "The Colour Out of Space," was directed by Daniel Haller, who had been Corman's art director on *The Haunted Palace.* Haller did revive the book in *The Dunwich Horror* (1970), produced by Corman, Nicholson, and Arkoff. It is one of the strangest films in the Lovecraft canon. If *Die, Monster, Die!* was a product of the Sixties with its jazzy rock score, garish special effects, and cheesy attempt at turning an aged Boris Karloff into a "monster" again, then *The Dunwich Horror* is a product of the swinging Seventies. Both a faithful adaptation of Lovecraft's writing and a ludicrous attempt at introducing the sexual mores and psychedelia of the period into a horror story, this film is a true curiosity. The screenplay, co-written by Curtis Hanson (who would go on to direct *L.A. Confidential, Wonder Boys,* and *8 Mile*), ignores the first half of Lovecraft's popular tale, in which Wilbur Whateley is born under mysterious circumstances and grows physically and mentally at an astonishing rate, causing turmoil in his family and terror in the town of Dunwich (think John Wyndham's *The Midwich Cuckoos,* the source novel for both versions of *Village of the Damned*). Instead, we meet Wilbur as an adult, and he is not the hideous, freakish giant described by Lovecraft. As portrayed by Dean Stockwell, Wilbur is a handsome seducer, as interested in corrupting Nancy Wagner (Sandra Dee, in a bold departure from her starring rôles in the innocuous Gidget and Tammy sequels) as he is in stealing *The Necronomicon* from the Miskatonic University library.

Wilbur's Van Helsing-like nemesis is Dr. Henry Armitage (Ed Begley), who organizes librarians and fellow scientists in the battle against Yog Sothoth. Lloyd Bochner plays Dr. Cory, Sam Jaffe (*Gunga Din*) plays Old Whateley, and Talia Shire has a cameo as a nurse. As in Lovecraft's story, a giant monster destroys barns and devours cattle; but since this was a low budget film, these attacks are accomplished through subjective camera work and choppy editing. The main creature — Wilbur's twin brother, long thought dead — is rather frightening the first time we see him, attacking and stripping a nurse who opens the wrong door: worm-like tentacles fill the screen to nauseating effect. But when the creature is viewed at the climax, the end result is about as convincing as King Gidorah in the old Godzilla films. With the twins laid to rest, Armitage helps Nancy off the altar upon which Wilbur nearly sacrificed her, and we see the image of a fetus nuzzling inside her belly! This nod to Roman Polanski and *Rosemary's Baby* brings this badly dated mess to an end. On the plus side, the score, "supervised" by Al Simms, is surprisingly cheerful, and the animated title sequence is entertaining.

The next film to open *The Necronomicon*'s pages was not a direct Lovecraft adaptation, but a project inspired by the author's works (just as Robert Bloch, August Derleth and others continued the "Cthulhu Mythos" on the printed page). Written and directed by Sam Raimi, and produced in 16mm on a budget of $300,000.00, *The Evil Dead* (1981) mixed aspects of Lovecraft, Richard Matheson's *I Am Legend,* and George Romero's *Night of the Living Dead* in a high-speed blender and splattered the screen with the results. Five college students spending a weekend in a remote cabin in the Michigan woods stumble upon a reel-to-reel tape recorder and a mysterious book bound in human flesh, both left there by a scientist who had recently returned from an archaeological expedition. When the students turn on the recorder, the archaeologist's recorded voice summons "Khandarian demons" that possess the hapless vacationers one by one. In the climax, bumbling hero Ash (Bruce Campbell) battles the book itself, which is neatly animated with grotesque features. Only "bodily dismemberment" can save the day, although the nihilistic ending casts doubt on that particular theory. The unseen archaeologist is a typical Lovecraft hero, and there is no doubt in this viewer's mind that the "Book of the Dead" is in fact *The Necronomicon*. When the demons are first summoned, a glowing red force rises from the ground outside the cabin, and the chilling effect can be described as "Lovecraftian." Certainly, H.P. never imagined the likes of Ash (Bruce Campbell) as a protagonist, but this film can be seen as a "next generation" spinoff of the author's material. Unrated and graphically violent, the film is scary as hell, and its black humor helped pave the way for Stuart Gordon's *Re-Animator* (1985), the first direct Lovecraft adaptation in fifteen years. Inventive camera work (subjective point-of-view shots from the demons in the woods actually recall those in *The Dunwich Horror*), no-holds-barred gore, and relentless pacing made this B picture a true cult classic.

Raimi and company returned with two sequels: *Evil Dead 2: Dead by Dawn* (1987), and *The Army of Darkness* (1993). The first, essentially a remake of the original film with a higher budget, more ambitious effects, and a "Three Stooges" slapstick mentality, begins with a prologue identifying *The Book of the Dead* as *The Necronomicon*. Neither Abdul Alhazred nor Cthulhu are named in the brief history, but the Old Ones are mentioned. The film ends with Ash reading an incantation from missing pages of the book and creating a vortex that catapults him through time to the Middle Ages (a similar effect was employed in Fred Dekker's imaginative 1987 monster mash, *The Monster Squad*).

The third film, even more comical than the second, follows Ash's Medieval misadventures fighting demons and creatures. The extent to which *The Necronomicon* has come to symbolize this trilogy became apparent when video distributor Anchor Bay Entertainment released a deluxe edition DVD of *Evil Dead 2*: the disk came packaged in a replica of *The Book of the Dead* which included latex "human skin" and illustrated pages straight out of the films.

Cast a Deadly Spell (1991), written by Joseph Dougherty, produced by Gale Anne Hurd, and directed by Martin Campbell for HBO, is an imaginative Lovecraft pastiche that illustrates the degree to which Lovecraft and his tome have achieved American pop cultural status. Fred Ward stars as Harry Philip Lovecraft, a private eye in a fantastical 1940s Los Angeles in which everyone but he uses magic. This clever film begins where Dashiell Hammett's *The Maltese Falcon* ended, and incorporates elements of Raymond Chandler's "The Big Sleep" (Lovecraft visits the estate of a wealthy, prospective employer, whose jailbait daughter rides a unicorn rather than a horse). In this alternate universe, Lovecraft is hired to locate *The Necronomicon,* which serves as the story's equivalent of Hammett's black bird — what Hitchcock called a "McGuffin." In the end, a villainous sorcerer summons a Cthulhu-like creature with disastrous results. Ward is comfortable as Lovecraft, and the hard-boiled dialogue has charm.

Paul Schrader directed a superior sequel, *Witch Hunt* (1994), also written by Dougherty, which recast Dennis Hopper as Lovecraft in a story set during the McCarthy era; *The Necronomicon* was not featured.

Also in 1994, Lovecraft and his book shared the spotlight in Brian Yuzna's *Necronomicon: Book of the Dead* (1994). After producing *Re-Animator* and *From Beyond* (1986), and directing *Bride of Re-Animator* (1990), Yuzna produced this anthology and directed two of the four tales included in it; Christophe Gans and Shusuke Kaneko directed the other two. Jeffrey Combs, who portrayed Herbert West and Crawford Tillinghast in Yuzna's previous Lovecraft adaptations, plays Lovecraft himself, with the aid of a prosthetic chin, in the wraparound segments. The co-stars of note are Tom Savini, Steve Johnson, and Screaming Mad George — special makeup effects artists who provided some of the outrageous creature effects.

In the wraparound segment, "The Library," Lovecraft, portrayed as a sword-cane-wielding action hero, reads segments from *The Necronomicon* before stealing it from a group of murderous monks. "The Drowned" is an original tale that offers a glimpse of Cthulhu at its climax; "The Cold" is an adaptation of "Cool Air," which was done better on Rod Serling's *Night Gallery* TV series, and "Whispers" is based on "The Whisperer in the Dark." Proving how sloppily constructed the film is, the wraparound segments occur in 1932, yet two of the three tales contained in the book that Lovecraft reads are set in the present! The film has decent production values, but lacks any sense of style, urgency, or logic.

It is as inevitable as Cthulhu's rising that other filmmakers will tackle the subject matter of Lovecraft's *The Necronomicon* again; after all, it's hard to put — or keep — a good book down. 🕷

Greg Lamberson's films, Slime City, New York Vampire, *and* Naked Fear *are due on DVD this year. His first novel,* Personal Demons, *recently appeared from Broken Umbrella Press.*

INNSMOUTH BANE

by John Glasby

illustrated by Allen Koszowski

I am writing this narrative in the sincere belief that something terrible has come to Innsmouth; something about which it is not wise to speak openly. Many of my neighbors, if they should ever read this account, will undoubtedly assume that any accusations I make against Obed Marsh are based upon jealousy since there is little doubt that he, alone, is prospering while those of us who lost much during the years of depression are still finding it difficult to profit from this strange upturn in fortune which is his alone.

My name is Jedediah Allen. My family left Boston and settled in Innsmouth in 1676, twenty-one years after the town was founded, my grandfather and father being engaged in trade with the Orient, prospering well following the success of the Revolution. The war of 1812, however, brought misfortune to many Innsmouth families. The loss of men and ships was heavy, the Gilman shipping business suffering particularly badly.

Only Obed Marsh seemed to have come out of the depression successfully. His three vessels, the *Sumatra Queen, Hetty,* and *Columbia* still made regular sailings to the islands of the South Seas. Yet there was, from the very beginning, something odd about these voyages. From the first, he returned with large quantities of gold trinkets, more treasure than anyone in Innsmouth had ever seen.

One rumor had it that this hoard of gold had been discovered by him concealed in some secret cave on Devil Reef, left there by buccaneers more than two centuries earlier; that he covertly ferried it ashore on nights when there was no moon. Yet having seen some of these artifacts for myself, for Obed displayed many of them quite openly, I was more inclined towards the former explanation as to their origin.

Certainly, the objects were beautiful in their intricate workmanship and design but this was marred by an alienness in their imagery. All of the objects appeared to have an aquatic motif. To my eye, they had disturbing suggestions of fish or frog symbols, totally unlike any of the Spanish trinkets from the West Indies.

There was also something strange about the metal from which they were fashioned which indicated a non-European source.

My attempts to get Obed to divulge any information about them all met with evasiveness. He would neither confirm nor deny any of the rumors.

There was one man, however, who might talk.

Matt Eliot, first mate on the *Sumatra Queen,* was known to frequent the inn on Water Street whenever he was in port and it was from him that I hoped to learn something.

It was two weeks before an opportunity presented itself. Entering the inn just after dark, I spotted Eliot in the far corner, among the shadows, and for once he appeared to be without his usual drinking companions. After purchasing two drinks, I walked over and sat in the chair opposite him. He clearly had had a lot to drink although the hour was still early.

I knew him to be a man of violent temper, readily aroused, one who had to be approached with caution and diplomacy.

Setting the drink down in front of him, I sat back and studied him closely for several moments. I wanted him to be sufficiently drunk to talk, but not too drunk to fall into a stupor. For a time, he gave no indication that he had noticed my presence. Then his hand went out for the glass and he took several swallows, wiping the back of his hand across his mouth.

Leaning forward, he peered closely at me. Then he grinned. "Jedediah Allen, ain't it?"

I nodded. "I'd like to talk with you, Matt," I said. "About these voyages you go on with Captain Marsh. Where'd he get all that gold? I'd like to buy some of it for myself."

His eyes opened and closed several times before he replied, "Reckon you'll have to speak to Obed about the gold. He keeps all of that for himself."

"But you do know where he gets it."

"O' course I do. Every man on those ships knows where that gold comes from." He leaned forward a little further, pushing his face up to mine, and dropping his voice to a hoarse whisper. "Every trip he makes, Obed sails for Othaheite. Couple o' years ago, we came across an island to the east not shown on any of our charts. The natives there, the Kanakys, worship some kind o' fish-god and they get all the fish and gold they want in exchange for sacrifices to this heathen god. Obed gives 'em beads and baubles for it."

He took another swallow of his drink. "There's somethin' else, somethin' —"

He broke off abruptly as if suddenly aware that he was on the point of saying something he shouldn't.

"Go on," I urged. "This is just between you and me, Matt."

"There's another island close to that where the Kanakys live. That's where they offer their sacrifices. Obed got me and two others to row him out there one night. God, it was horrible. Not just the ruins that looked as if they'd lain on the bottom of the sea for millions of years, but what we heard and saw while we were there, on the other side of the island. Things comin' up out o' the sea like fish and frogs, only they walked on two legs like men, croakin' and whistlin' like demons."

I saw him shudder at the memory. "Obed never went back to that accursed island again. I reckon even he was scared by what we saw."

Finishing my drink, I thanked him for his information and left. As a staunch member of the Baptist Church, I knew that it was my duty to warn others of Marsh's activities. But without proof, it was doubtful if I would be even listened to. Obed was a prominent figure in town and after all, it had long been an established practice for sea captains to exchange goods with the natives of these far-flung islands. Before I could tell anyone, I needed to know a lot more about what Obed was bringing into Innsmouth apart from gold.

It was then I decided to wait for his return from his latest voyage. I already knew that both the *Betty* and the *Columbia* had sailed some seven months previously, leaving the *Sumatra Queen* tied up at the harbor for repairs.

Over the next few weeks, I made discreet inquiries concerning these ships and finally ascertained they were due off Innsmouth some five weeks later. I had already decided upon the best vantage point to maintain a close watch on any activity without exposing myself to view. Accordingly, on the night in question, I made my way along Water Street to the harbor. The night was dark and starlit with no moon and I let myself into one of the large warehouses lining the waterfront.

After going up to one of the upper storeys, I crouched down by the window from where I had a clear and unrestricted view of the entire harbor. Although dark, there was sufficient starlight for me to readily make out the irregular black outline of Devil Reef perhaps a mile and a half away.

It was almost midnight when I spotted the two ships rounding Kingsport Head. The *Columbia* was in the lead with the *Hetty* about half a mile astern. Twenty minutes later, after following the movements of the two vessels closely, it became apparent that Marsh meant to bring them both into the harbor rather than anchor offshore.

By the time the vessels had docked a further hour had passed. There was much activity on both ships and the tall figure of Captain Marsh was clearly visible. By shifting my position slightly, I was able to watch closely as the cargoes were unloaded onto the quayside. Much of it consisted of large bales, which were carried into the warehouse adjacent to that in which I had concealed myself. There was little talk among the men, much of the work being carried out in complete silence. After a while, the crews vanished along Water Street and only Marsh and one crewman were left on board the *Columbia.*

When they eventually disembarked they were carrying a large chest between them and it was this, I guessed, that contained more of the gold which Marsh was bringing back from that unnamed island in the South Seas.

I now had ample confirmation as to the source of this gold and had Marsh continued merely with smuggling such trinkets, there was little that could be said against him. Prior to the war, during the privateering days, such activities were

commonplace in Innsmouth and were certainly not frowned upon by the townsfolk.

By now Marsh seemed to have fully accepted this pagan religion of those natives with whom he traded on a regular basis. He began to speak out vociferously against all of the religious communities, urging anyone who would listen to abandon their Christian faith and worship this pagan god, promising them wealth beyond their wildest dreams if they did so.

Had we all listened to the Reverend Joseph Wallingham who entreated his congregation to have nothing to do with those who worshipped pagan gods and worldly goods; had I known then what I was to discover the next time the *Sumatra Queen* returned from that accursed island, all of the ensuing madness might have been averted.

But few heeded the Reverend Wallingham and it was a further year before that fateful night when the *Sumatra Queen* docked. It is hard to say what gave me the notion that Obed Marsh was smuggling something more than gold into Innsmouth, nor what brought to my mind the recollection of the old tunnels beneath the town, leading from the sea into the very center of Innsmouth.

But remember them I did. For two nights, I concealed myself on top of the cliff overlooking the shore but without any untoward happenings. On the third night, however, a little before midnight, I observed a party of men moving along the beach from the direction of the harbor. It was clear the men believed themselves to be safe from prying eyes for they carried lanterns and as they drew near the entrance to one of the tunnels, almost immediately below my hiding place, I recognized Obed Marsh in the lead with Matt Eliot and five of the crew close behind.

But it was the sight of the others accompanying them that sent a shiver of nameless dread through me so that I almost cried out. Without doubt they were natives brought back from that terrible island and even in the dim light cast by the bobbing lanterns, I could see there was something distinctly inhuman about them.

Their heads were curiously distorted with long, sloping foreheads, outthrust jaws and bulging eyes like those of a frog or fish. Their gait, too, was peculiar as if they were hopping rather than walking.

Trembling and shaking, I lay there and watched as the party entered the tunnel mouth and disappeared. Not until a full half hour had passed was I able to push myself to my feet and stagger back into town.

God alone knew how many of those creatures Marsh had smuggled into Innsmouth under the unsuspecting noses of the population, concealing them somewhere in his mansion on Washington Street.

At the time, I could tell no one. Marsh had too tight a hold on all who sailed with him for any of them to talk. What dire purpose lay behind this wholesale importation of these natives, I couldn't begin to guess. I knew full well there had to be a reason, but Marsh kept it to himself and none of the creatures were ever seen on the town streets, even after dark.

Over the next two years, whenever he was in town, Marsh continued his tirade against the established churches; and when several of the leading churchmen unaccountably disappeared, it became abundantly clear that he intended to become the only force in Innsmouth and those who did not join him also had a tendency to vanish in peculiar circumstances or were driven out of the town.

Then, suddenly and without warning, disaster struck Innsmouth. A terrible epidemic swept through the town, a disease for which there seemed no remedy. Hundreds, including my own wife, died during the outbreak. The few doctors could do nothing to stem the spread of the disease, merely declaring that it was one of foreign origin they had never encountered before. Almost certainly, they maintained, it had been brought into Innsmouth by one of the vessels trading with the Orient.

The dead and dying were everywhere. There was no escape since the Federal authorities, on hearing of it, quarantined the entire town and surrounding region. By the time the contagion had burnt itself out almost half of the population had succumbed.

Now, for the first time, I spoke out of what I had witnessed that night on the cliffs. Other townsfolk then came forward to tell of curious foreigners glimpsed in the fog, particularly along the waterfront at dead of night, some swimming strongly out to sea in the direction of Devil Reef, and many more coming in the other direction.

We knew that something had to be done and a

meeting was hurriedly convened to discuss the rapidly deteriorating situation. There, it was agreed that no other course of action was open to us but to raid the Marsh mansion. Further action would depend upon what we found there. It was essential, of course, that no intimation of this plan should reach Obed for there were now several of the townsfolk who appeared to have thrown in their lot with him.

Two Federal investigators, agents Jensen and Corder, were present at the meeting and although at first reluctant to support this taking of the law into our own hands, they eventually agreed to lead the raid. One group, led by Jensen, would go in at the front while agent Corder would command the second which would enter by the rear.

Arming myself with a pistol, I accompanied the second group. In all, we numbered twenty-two men. None of us knew what to expect as we made our way silently along Lafayette Street towards the rear of the huge building. Once we were in place, we waited for the two blasts on a whistle, which would signal that the other band was ready to move in.

Lights were visible in three of the rear windows and occasionally a shadow would pass across the curtains. Clearly, the house was occupied but whether the shadows we saw belonged to members of the Marsh family or to servants, it was impossible to tell.

The signal to attack came five minutes later. Running forward, three of the men smashed in the heavy door and moments later, we were inside the house. A long, gloomy corridor led through the house towards the front of the building. Several rooms opened off from it on either side but a quick search revealed only two terrified servants and little out of the ordinary.

Meeting up with the first group we found Obed Marsh seated in a chair before the fire. He had obviously attempted to reach for a weapon when the men had burst in, for a pistol lay on the table. Now he sat covered by the revolver in Jensen's hand.

"Did you find anything?" Jensen spoke directly to Corder.

"Nothing in any of the back rooms," Corder replied. "But if there is any contraband here, it's likely to be well hidden."

"You'll find nothing!" Marsh snarled. He half rose to his feet, then sat down again at a gesture from Jensen. "And you'll all pay for this unwarranted intrusion. I'll make damned sure of that."

There was something in his threat that sent a shiver through me. I had long known him to be a man who never made idle threats.

While the rest of the men made a thorough search of the other room with five of them climbing the stairs to the upper storeys, I made a slow circuit of the room. Several portraits of the Marsh family members, going back for several generations, hung on the walls but it was not these that made me feel uneasy. There were also other things, lining the mantel piece above the wide hearth and on top of several long shelves around the walls.

There could be only one place where Marsh could have obtained them. Grotesque statues depicting hideous monstrosities, the likes of which I had never seen before. In particular, I came across a trio of statuettes, each about ten inches in height, which were frightful in the extreme. Apart from the nightmarish contours, which appeared to be hybrids of various sea creatures, the anatomical quintessence of these idols, the grotesque tentacular nature of the limbs and malformed torsos, suggested to me things from some distant pre-human era. The nature of the material from which they were fashioned was also highly peculiar. A pale, nauseous green, striated with minute black lines, it was extremely heavy and none of us could even hazard a guess as to what it was.

A sudden shout from one of the adjoining rooms jerked my attention from them. In a loose bunch, we made our way towards the sound, leaving Jensen to keep an eye on Marsh.

In one of the rooms, the men had come across a locked door which, on being broken down, revealed a flight of stone steps, clearly leading to cellars beneath the house. Lighting three of the lanterns we had brought with us, we descended the steps, almost retching on the stench which came up to meet us. It was a sharp, fishy odor, which caught at the backs of our throats, almost suffocating us.

At the bottom, in the pale light from our lanterns, we saw the shocking confirmation of what I had said earlier concerning my nocturnal vigils on the cliffs. There were more than a score of natives crowded into the cellar and one or two of the men cried out as we tried to assimilate what we saw.

Several of us had sailed to many foreign ports during the prosperous trading and privateering days and were fully conversant with the many native races found on different islands of the Pacific. But what we saw in the wavering lantern light was something none of us had ever witnessed!

These were the most repulsive creatures I had ever set eyes on. Apart from some curious deformity of their bodies, their bulging eyes and oddly shaped heads held something of the aquatic physiognomy of fishes and I could swear that some of them had hands and feet which seemed to be webbed!

Sickened by the sight and smell, I turned away and it was then I noticed the hastily boarded-up doorway in the far wall where the shadows were thickest. Drawing Corder's attention to it, we soon ripped away the boards and shone the light of one of the lanterns into the gaping aperture that lay behind them. There was no doubting what it was; the opening into one of the old smugglers' tunnels leading down towards the sea.

"So that's how he brought them here," Corder muttered grimly. "God alone knows how many more of these creatures are in the town, probably concealed in cellars like this."

Charged the next day with illegally importing unidentified aliens, Obed Marsh and several of his crew were thrown into jail to await trial and for two days thereafter an uneasy quiet reigned in Innsmouth.

It was not to last, however. For then came the day which was to change Innsmouth forever.

As far as I was concerned, my suspicions were aroused when I noticed several groups of men in the streets adjoining the jail. All of them were either men who had sailed with Marsh in the past or those who had joined him later when he had spoken out against the various religious denominations.

It was clear their intention was to secure Obed's release by force and this seemed confirmed when they began moving in the direction of Main Street. Hurriedly alerting several of my neighbors and telling them to spread the word, we succeeded in gathering more than fifty men armed with muskets, pikes, knives and any other weapons they could lay their hands on.

By the time we reached the jail we found it had already come under attack. Some of the raiders had forced their way inside and the unmistakable sound of shots came from somewhere within the building. Moments later, we were set upon by the yelling mob and I was fighting for my life against men I had known for years who now acted like crazed madmen.

For a time, since we outnumbered them by almost two to one, we succeeded in driving them back from their objective. But as they retreated along Main Street, a great horde of natives burst out of Waite Street, forcing us back towards the bridge over the Manuxet.

In the distance, I could clearly pick out more gunfire coming from all directions but concentrated mainly near the center of the town and along the waterfront and guessed that fighting had broken out in several places. Already, we had suffered a number of casualties: seven men had been killed and almost twice that number wounded.

Luckily, the majority of the natives were unarmed, relying on sheer weight of numbers to overwhelm us. Several were killed within the first few minutes but the rest came on, heedless of their casualties.

It was the bridge that temporarily saved us. On either side, the riverbank as far as the falls, was far too steep and treacherous to be readily scaled and the Manuxet was in full flood after the recent rains, thereby preventing the creatures from crossing the river and assaulting us from the rear.

For almost an hour we managed to hold off the attackers, inflicting terrible carnage among their ranks. When they began to pull back, we believed we had beaten them off and although firing could still be heard around the town center, it was sporadic, and it appeared the situation was slowly being brought under control.

After what several of us had witnessed in the

cellar below the Marsh mansion, I think we believed we were prepared for anything. But nothing could have prepared us for what came next.

It was Silas Benson who suddenly called our attention to the river below us. As I have said, the Manuxet was in full flood but now it teemed with black shapes, swimming upstream against the racing current. That they had come from the sea was immediately obvious. Literally hundreds of them came swarming onto the bank and one horrified glance was enough to show that these creatures were even less human than those we had stumbled upon earlier.

Hopping in a manner hideously suggestive of frogs, they clambered up the steep sides with ease. There was no chance of defeating such a multitude and our only hope of survival was to flee, across the bridge, and along Main Street. Another bank of natives, surging out of Dock Street, attempted to halt us and our ammunition was almost spent by the time we broke through them. Four more of our number were killed before we reached the relative safety of my house where we barricaded ourselves in.

By now it was abundantly clear that those monsters from the sea had taken over the whole of the town. Sporadic firing could still be heard in the distance but we all knew that further resistance was futile.

By the morning of the next day, after spending the night confined to the house, we finally pieced together the full story of what had happened. Obed Marsh and those imprisoned with him had been released.

Both of the Federal investigators who had accompanied us to the Marsh mansion had been slaughtered. John Lawrence, editor of the *Innsmouth Courier* on Dock Street, who had often spoken out against Marsh, had been dragged into the street and murdered. The presses and printing equipment had been smashed and the offices set on fire.

Thus it was that Obed Marsh now controlled the whole of Innsmouth. His word was law. Within weeks, the old Masonic Temple on Federal Street had been taken over and replaced by the Esoteric Order of Dagon.

Only a handful of the townsfolk were allowed to leave Innsmouth. These were mostly Lithuanians and Poles. Whether Marsh considered that no one outside Innsmouth would believe anything of what they said about the town or whether, not being descendants of the original

settlers, he adjudged them to be of no importance, no one knew. After they had gone, those who remained were allowed to join the Esoteric Order of Dagon. There were few who declined.

It was not only the gold which made people join this new religion Marsh had brought back with him, nor the fact that, by now, most folk were mortally afraid of him. What persuaded the majority to join was that Marsh promised all who joined that, if they took his five oaths and obeyed him implicitly, they would never die.

When I was asked to join, I refused, as did my son. I had read sufficient reports concerning the rites that had been practiced in nearby Arkham during the witch trials to know that similar inducements had been made then, that all who worshipped Satan would be granted eternal life. At the time, I knew it to be nothing more than myth and superstition, merely an enticement to get people to join in their unholy rites.

Now, however, I know differently. It soon became apparent that Marsh was involved with those deep ones much more deeply than was first thought. In return for their continued aid, he declared that the townspeople must mate with these creatures. He, himself, was forced to take a wife from among them although she was never seen abroad and no one was able to tell who — or what — she was.

All of that happened almost twenty years ago. More and more of the folk, particularly the younger ones, acquired the same look as many of those natives we had found in Marsh's cellar and some, as the years passed, were even worse, being little different from those creatures which had come from the sea to take over the town. Almost all of the Marsh, Gilman, Hogg, and Brewster families were affected by this Innsmouth look. Curiously, Ephraim Waite's family

remained untainted even though he was one of Marsh's closest acquaintances.

Rumor had it, however, that Waite had once resided in Arkham and had a reputation as a wizard, some even suggesting that he was the same warlock as was present before and during the witch trials there, two centuries earlier. That this was nothing more than idle gossip, spread by those who were more afraid of him than of Obed Marsh, seemed undeniable.

It was now becoming more difficult and dangerous for me to keep watch on Marsh's activities. Even though the deep ones had returned to the sea shortly after Marsh's release from jail, a score of years before, those who bore the Innsmouth look were in the majority and any of the population untouched by it were kept under close scrutiny.

Only those who belonged to the Order were allowed in the vicinity of the Esoteric Order of Dagon Hall. Nevertheless, on a number of occasions I managed to approach within fifty yards of it under cover of darkness. Even on those nights when there was no service taking place, the building was never silent. Strange echoes seemed to come from somewhere deep beneath the foundations; weird sounds like nothing I had heard before.

But things were worse whenever a service was being held. Just to see some of those who attended made me want to turn and run. Scaled things that wore voluminous clothing to conceal the true shapes of what lay beneath, walking upright like men but with a horrible hopping gait that set my teeth on edge. And the chanting which came from within was something born out of nightmare. Harsh gutturals such as could never have been uttered by normal human throats; croaks and piping whistles, more reminiscent of the frogs and whippoorwills in the hills around Arkham than anything remotely approaching human speech.

Dear Lord — that such blasphemies as those

could exist in this sane, everyday world! I found myself on the point of believing some of the tales spread abroad in Innsmouth concerning some deep undersea city, millions of years old, lying on the ocean floor just beyond Devil Reef. When I had first heard them from Elijah Winton, I had immediately dismissed them as the ravings of a madman. But hearing those hideous sounds emanating from the Temple of Dagon made me think again.

Something unutterably evil and terrible lay out there where the sea bed reputedly fell sheer for more than two thousand feet into the abyssal depths. Whatever it was, from whatever internal regions it had come, it now held Obed Marsh and his followers in its unbreakable grip.

Then, two days ago, I found myself wandering along Water Street alongside the harbor. What insane compulsion led me in that direction I could not guess. I knew I was being kept under close surveillance all of the way; that eyes were marking my every move.

Where the sense of imminent danger came from it was impossible to tell, nor was it any actual sound. Rather it was a disturbing impression of movement in the vicinity of Marsh Street and Fish Street. I could see nothing to substantiate this but the sensation grew more pronounced as I halted at a spot where it was possible to look out over the breakwater to where Devil Reef thrust its sinister outline above the water.

It was several minutes before I realized there was something different about the contours of that black reef. I had seen it hundreds of times in the past; I knew its outlines like the back of my hand. But now it seemed far higher than normal, almost as if the sea level around it had fallen substantially.

And then I recognized the full, soul-destroying horror of what I was seeing. That great mass of rock was unchanged. What distorted it was something huge and equally black, which was rising from the sea behind it.

Shuddering convulsively, unable to move a single muscle, I could only stand there, my gaze fixed immutably upon that — *thing* — which rose out of the water until it loomed high above Devil Reef. Mercifully, much of its tremendous bulk lay concealed by the rock and the ocean. Had it all been visible I am certain I would have lost what remained of my sanity in that horror-crazed instant.

There was the impression of a mass of writhing tentacles surrounding a vast, bulbous head, of what looked like great wings outspread behind the shoulders, and a mountainous bulk hidden by the reef. It dripped with great strands of obnoxious seaweed. I knew that, even from that distance, it was aware of me with a malevolent intensity. And there was something more — an aura of utter malignancy which vibrated in the air, filling my mind with images of nightmarish horror.

This, then, was the quintessence of all the evil which had come to Innsmouth; the embodiment of the abomination which Captain Obed Marsh had wittingly, or inadvertently, brought to the town in exchange for gold.

I remember little of my nightmare flight along Marsh Street and South Street. My earliest coherent memory is of slamming and bolting my door and standing, shivering violently, in the hallway. I had thought those creatures which now shambled along the streets of Innsmouth were the final symbolism of evil in this town but that monstrosity I had witnessed out in the bay was infinitely worse.

What mad perversity of nature had produced it, where it had originated, and what its terrible purpose might be, I dreaded to think. I knew it could be none other than Dagon, that pagan god these people now worshipped. I also recognized that I now knew too much, that neither Obed Marsh, nor the deep ones which infested the waters around Innsmouth, could ever allow me to leave and tell of what I had witnessed.

There is only one course open to me. I have set down everything in this narrative and I intend to conceal it where only my son, now serving with the North in the war which has torn our country apart, can find it.

Through my window I can see the dark, mis-shapen figures now massing outside, and it is not difficult to guess at their intentions. Very soon, they will come to break down the door.

I have to be silenced, and possibly sacrificed, so that the Esoteric Order of Dagon may continue to flourish and the worship of Dagon may go on unhindered.

But I shall thwart whatever plans they have for me. My revolver lies in front of me on the table and there is a single bullet still remaining in the chamber!

✍ *John Stephen Glasby was born in 1928, and graduated from Nottingham University with an honors degree in Chemistry. He started his career as a research chemist for I.C.I. in 1952, and worked for them until his retirement. Over the next two decades, he began a parallel career as an extraordinarily prolific writer of science-fiction novels and short stories, his first novels appearing in the summer of 1952. Always a great fan of H.P. Lovecraft, Glasby wrote a collection of Mythos stories which August Derleth commissioned for Arkham House. Derleth suggested extensive revisions and improvements, which Glasby duly followed. Unfortunately, Derleth died before the collection could be published, and the book was returned to Glasby. "Innsmouth Bane" is one of those pastiches.*

SIEGE

Clouds — great, gray
amongst the top that cling to spires
of kingdom's high-walled castle

Dragons fly
swoop through the gray
yet hold for now their fire at bay

Come Knights, come Templar, Magic Wielders
lay down the gate
bear 'cross the moat
t'ward doom or gallant victory
one outcome based on fate

Dragon's nostril, breath of fire
display together mighty ire . . .

Horse and rider ready now
The gates and moat well lined
with Gypsy, Witch, and Shaman-Wizard
Grand staffs of magic primed

Clouds — great, gray
evaporates — The Sun!
Away with Dragon's fiery tongue
their camouflage undone!

Oh, happy day in kingdom great
no storms of violence as of late
And merry queens with children two
have not a care, no wounds, no woe

— Lynne Jamneck

A TALK WITH RICHARD MATHESON

by Michael McCarty

Richard Matheson is a legend in the speculative fiction field. He has been called "one of the most important writers of the 20th century" by Ray Bradbury, and his work has inspired the giants of the genre such as Stephen King, who names Matheson as "the author who influenced me most as a writer," and Dean Koontz, who says, "We're all a lot richer to have Richard Matheson."

Many of his classic novels have been turned into major motion pictures: *I Am Legend* (filmed twice, as *The Last Man On Earth,* and *The Omega Man*), *Bid Time Return* (filmed as *Somewhere In Time*), *What Dreams May Come, A Stir of Echoes, The Shrinking Man* (filmed as *The Incredible Shrinking Man*), and *Hell House* (filmed as *The Legend Of Hell House*).

He also wrote the scripts for some of the most memorable episodes of *The Twilight Zone, Star Trek,* and *Night Gallery.* His screenplays for television also include *The Night Stalker, The Night Strangler, Dracula, Dead of Night, Duel* and *Trilogy of Terror.* With a career spanning over five decades, Matheson has won awards from the World Science Fiction Convention (the Hugo), the World Fantasy Convention, and the Writer's Guild, as well as the Bram Stoker Lifetime Achievement Award, the Edgar Allan Poe Award, and The Golden Spur.

His latest book is *The Kolchak Scripts,* published by Gauntlet Press. It is a collection of all three screenplays he wrote for TV movies (*The Night Killers* was co-written with William F. Nolan).

Michael McCarthy: Next year will mark the 50th anniversary of *I Am Legend.* When you were writing that novel, did you imagine it would still be popular five decades later? What do you think contributes to the novel's longevity?

Richard Matheson: No, I never dreamed it would do that. If it is attributable to anything, it would be because it's a good story. It's an interesting story. It's an approach to vampires that wasn't taken before. Actually, although most people doubt it — I think it is the only genuine science-fiction book I have written. I base the book on psychology and physical facts — that are actually so. It seems to make sense to me.

Q: Is the title *I Am Legend* a Biblical reference to the Book of Mark, "I am legion"?

Matheson: No, I just made it up. Sometimes when they review it, they call it, *I Am a Legend* which destroys the rhythm of it.

Q: Is there going to be a 50th anniversary of the book next year? Is there a third movie still being made?

Matheson: I don't know. Maybe Barry Hoffman of Gauntlet Press, who put out a very nice edition, will re-issue it.

They keep talking about it. One night I ran across *Night of The Living Dead,* and thought "Oh you son of a gun, you." I was working on a story idea that I had for George Romero when he met me. He backed off, holding his arms up for protection and said, "It never made any money."

I don't know what's the point of making the movie. They never made it the way it should have been made. They just keep getting further away each time. Some guy wrote a script — it was a good script, but it was totally removed from my book. I don't think there will be any vampires any more. Not from my book any more.

Q: In the summer of 1950, when you were 23 years old, your story "Born of Man and Woman" appeared in the third issue of *The Magazine of Fantasy & Science Fiction* — and two years after *I Am Legend* was published, *The Incredible Shrinking Man,* which was a screenplay by you based on your book *The Shrinking Man,* hit the silver screen. Was that an exciting time for you? In a period of six years you went from a short story to a movie.

Matheson: I wanted to call the movie *The Shrinking Man* to have some kind of a metaphor, but they changed that. I was disappointed with the film for many years. I began to appreciate it more and realize it was very unusual for its time.

Q: Several of your novels have been adapted to the silver screen since *The Incredible Shrinking Man.* What are some of your favorite movies based on your work?

Matheson: I liked *The Comedy of Terrors,* that Jacques Tourneur directed for American International Pictures. It had the grand old-timers in it — Vincent Price, Boris Karloff, Peter Lorre, Basil Rathbone and Joyce Jameson. I liked that very much. *Somewhere in Time,* of course — that turned out very satisfying.

Most of my satisfying films were on television.

There was *Duel*, Steven Spielberg's first film. There was *The Night Stalker, The Night Stranger*. There was *The Morning After,* with Dick Van Dyke, about alcoholism — which I think is a marvelous piece of work. There was *The Dreamer of Oz* about the writing of the *Wizard of Oz*. John Ritter played L. Frank Baum. There's *Dying Room Only* — I've said this many times, it's the only film I ever had that got better than it deserved.

Q: Are there any other Richard Matheson books that Hollywood is currently interested in?

Matheson: Spielberg is supposed to be reading a screenplay that I wrote from my last novel, which was published last year, which they called *Hunted Past Reason* — which I wanted to call *To Live*. I don't know why they changed it. That is the first time a publisher has done that to me. I called the screenplay *To Live*.

Q: *The Kolchak Scripts* from Gauntlet Press had three of your TV movie scripts: *The Night Stalker, The Night Strangler* and *The Night Killers* (which you co-wrote with William F. Nolan). *The Night Killers* was never filmed. What can you tell us about that script?

Matheson: The main reason it wasn't filmed was because Dan Curtis and Darren McGavin had become alienated so that killed it right there. They were also in the works for setting up the *Kolchak: The Night Stalker* series. They didn't want to do another TV movie — it was too bad. It had an idea, for its time, that was very unique. It has become terribly hackneyed as the years went by — which is the idea of famous political figures being replaced by androids. It was a new idea at the time and it was very funny. It takes place in Hawaii.

Q: *The Night Stalker,* when it aired January 11, 1972, had over 75 million viewers, making it one of the highest rated TV movies of its time. Did that surprise you, that the show would be so popular?

Matheson: Sure, but it surprised everybody. It was very well done. But I don't think anybody expected that.

Q: Over the years, there have been a lot of comparisons of *Kolchak* and *The X-Files*. What are your thoughts on the subject?

Matheson: Chris Carter has admitted openly that his series was inspired by *Kolchak*. He even had a Senator Richard Matheson as a character in one of the shows. He was the one Senator who sympathized with the *X-Files* program. Chris Carter has agreed to write an introduction for *The Kolchak Scripts*.

Q: You worked with Dan Curtis on several projects. Why do you think you guys work so well

together?

Matheson: He liked my writing very much. We got along. Although he has a temper, he never showed it to me or Bill Nolan, who has also worked with him. Dan has an excellent sense of humor — which tapered off any kind of tense moment there might be. He has a very good story sense. He is very willing to communicate with you. He is also a marvelous director.

Q: What is the most perfect Richard Matheson book you have written?

Matheson: *Bid Time Return,* filmed as *Somewhere in Time*. It's probably the best-written book that I have ever done. *What Dreams May Come* is the most telling, the most important — if you want to call it that. Those are in the later series of books. I'd also put in *I Am Legend, The Shrinking man,* and *Hunted Past Reason*.

Q: Was *Abu and the 7 Marvels* fun to write?

Matheson: Yes. It just won the Benjamin Franklin Award for the best published Child's Book Of The Year, as much to Barry Hoffman's and Bill Stout's credit as to mine.

Q: Wasn't Bill Nolan originally involved with *Abu and the 7 Marvels*?

Matheson: The title page when I submitted it, said, "novel by Richard Matheson, story by Richard Matheson and William F. Nolan." If the book goes into a second printing, publisher Barry Hoffman promised that would go on the title page.

Q: You lived and wrote for the most part of the 20th century and now we are in the 21st century. What do you think are humanity's prospects in the 21st century? How do you see the world heading along from here?

Matheson: I put together a book called *The Path*. It included all the quotations of the man who I regarded as one of the most important metaphysicians of the 20th century, named Harold Percival. As I wrote in the introduction, I felt that the last decade of the 20th century was the most important in the history of mankind. Man had to come to the realization of what he really is and what he represents in life or things were going to go really bad. Things are going really bad.

Q: You have written in an astounding variety of genres, yet you are renowned for your science fiction and horror. What is it that science fiction and horror does that mainstream literature can't do?

Matheson: A straight-line novel is more demanding. The films now are mostly based on comic books. There are some wonderful adult movies being made, but they all are being made by independents which usually only make a few dollars before disappearing.

The genre appeals to younger fans, where there is not that for straight novels.

Q: You expanded a quartet of Edgar Allan Poe's work for Roger Corman — American International Pictures. How was it, writing adaptations of Poe for the silver screen?

Matheson: The first, *The House of Usher* came closest to the story but even that had to be expanded. As it went on, the deviation became more extreme all the time. Finally, I got tired of writing about people buried alive. I had to make a joke out of it, which was *The Comedy of Terrors.*

The Raven, supposedly based on a poem by Edgar Allan Poe, was rather far removed. "The Pit & The Pendulum" is a very short story about a guy on a torture table during the Spanish Inquisition and "The Raven" was just a poem. And I had to make those into full length films — it absolutely required that I make up a story.

Q: You've collaborated with your son Richard Christian Matheson. What is the secret of a successful collaboration?

Matheson: You have to think similarly. To collaborate is usually very easy in the beginning. When Richard and I put together a story, it comes together very quickly, because we both saw things the same way. The difficulty comes when you're doing the writing. His style and my style are quite different — he has become a much better writer than I am. He's brilliant.

Q: You have a very talented family.

Matheson: Yes. Richard has a script now that is going to be made into a pilot film for *Showtime,* and they just signed Frank Pierson to direct it. It's about an evangelical family. They are going to shoot it in Utah this summer. It is an absolutely brilliant script called *Paradise.*

My daughter Ali and her husband are also very successful writers. They live in Vancouver, Canada. They sold a pilot which is going to be shot this summer. Originally they had a commitment for 88 hour-films. Now, sensibly it's down to 22.

My son Christian is also an excellent writer, who is with his former and now again partner Ed Solomon, who wrote *Men In Black*. They wrote the "Bill & Ted" films together. He's now working on a musical about Joseph Smith, the founder of the Mormons. Martha Davis from The Motels has written songs for it. He has also written a marvelous script called *Wallace In Wonderland.* They are all very, very talented.

Q: Do you have any anecdotes about your friend William Nolan that you would care to share?

Matheson: I have known Bill for fifty years. He was in the original California group of Charles Beaumont, Ray Russell, Ray Bradbury, George Clayton Johnson, and myself. Bill is very inventive, he has written very interesting stories and books, he has a major study about Dashiell Hammett, which he is just finishing up on for some major publisher. He's written a lot of non-fiction books, which he is really good at. He worked for Dan Curtis on a number of projects including *The Turn of the Screw* and *Doctor Jekyll & Mr. Hyde.*

He's a great artist as well. When I first met him, I used to go over to his house. He studied at an art institute for a long time. He has some beautiful oil paintings. Whenever he writes me a note, he'll dash off a little cartoon, which is just marvelous. Ray Bradbury and William Stout are also great at that.

Art talent is something completely out of my world. I admire it, but I can't do it.

Q: Any advice to beginning writers?

Matheson: To aspiring writers, I have the same thing to say that Ray Bradbury has said for years. It's nice to have encouragement. Ray was very encouraging to me at the beginning. But, fundamentally, writing classes, writing seminars can be a waste of time. If you want to be a writer, you've just got to sit down by yourself in a quiet room . . . or some writers, like my son Richard, put on music to do it with — I could never do that . . . and you just have to *write*. Bradbury says, "God bless you, write 52 stories a year." You'll certainly be a much better writer than you were at the beginning of the year. You can be inspired by various writers. We were all inspired by Bradbury at the beginning, we were all pseudo-Bradburys. But we all evolved our own styles. But that is what it all comes down to: writing, writing, writing. It's the only way.

Books by Richard Matheson:

Fury on Sunday (1953)
Someone Is Bleeding (1953)
I Am Legend (1954)
The Shrinking Man (1956)

A Stir of Echoes (1958)
Ride the Nightmare (1959)
Hell House (1971)
Bid Time Return (1975)

A TALK WITH RICHARD MATHESON

What Dreams May Come (1978)
Earthbound (1982 & 1989)
Journal of the Gun Years (1991)
The Path (1993)
7 Steps to Midnight (1993)
The Gun Fight (1993)
Shadow on the Sun (1994)

Now You See It . . . (1995)
Hunger and Thirst (2000)
Camp Pleasant (2001)
Abu and the 7 Marvels (2002)
Hunted Past Reason (2002)
Come Fygures, Come Shadows (2003)

Collections by Richard Matheson:

Born of Man and Woman (1954)
The Shores of Space (1957)
Shock! (1961)
Shock 2 (1964)
Shock 3 (1966)
Shock 4 (1970)
Shockwaves (1970)
Richard Matheson's Twilight Zone Scripts (1986)

Richard Matheson Collected Stories (1989)
By the Gun (1993)
Nightmare at 20,000 Feet (2000)
California Sorcery (with William F. Nolan) (2001)
Duel (2002)
Off Beat: Uncollected Stories (2002)
A Primer of Reality (2002)
Richard Matheson's Kolchak Scripts (2003)

✍ *Michael McCarty is the author of* Giants of the Genre, *a collection of interviews of the greats of science fiction, fantasy, and horror, published by Wildside Press. He lives in Rock Island, Illinois, and is currently shopping around his vampire novel,* Liquid Diet.

He has been a fan of Richard Matheson since his teens after reading I Am Legend.

THE MESSENGER

H. P. Lovecraft

The thing, he said, would come in the night at three
From the old churchyard on the hill below;
But crouching by an oak fire's wholesome glow,
I tried to tell myself it could not be.

Surely, I mused, it was pleasantry
Devised by one who did not truly know
The Elder Sign, bequeathed from long ago,
That sets the fumbling forms of darkness free.

He had not meant it — no — but still I lit
Another lamp as starry Leo climbed
Out of the Seekonk, and a steeple chimed
Three — and the firelight faded, bit by bit.

Then at the door that cautious rattling came —
And the mad truth devoured me like a flame!

HE WANTED TO LIVE

by Richard Matheson

illustrated by Alex McVey

And in the early morning when he had just about managed to fall into a troubled sleep — Lucy woke him up.

He was all curled up like a fetus in one corner of their bed. He jumped when she touched him. He jumped as if he'd been stabbed. He stared at her in terror. He wanted to shout at her — Don't you dare come near me! She was used to his nerves and she didn't know it was more than nerves now. She said — Breakfast — and she went out of the bedroom.

He lay back on the pillow and looked at the ceiling with hopeless resignation. He looked until his heart slowed down and his hands stopped shaking. He looked out of the window at the gray silence of another morning. Another day. Another collection of wracking hours.

The process began. His brain had hardly dragged itself from darkness. But it started to leave him. He couldn't control it. It thought everything he didn't want it to think.

There was the ceiling and there were the walls. Look at that crack in the ceiling. Suppose the roof gave. Suppose the attic with its dusty forgotten contents showered down on him. Suppose he were crushed as he lay there, the stored-away relics breaking every bone. Maybe the house would catch fire. Lucy was in the kitchen. She gets careless. A flame shoots out from the stove. Ignition. Conflagration.

He dressed and he was afraid. He might catch a germ from the clothes. The tie, the shirt, the coat might get caught in some machinery somewhere — who knew where. It might twist his flesh and cut off his breath, make his veins and arteries stand out in stark relief like pulsing tubes of blue spaghetti. His shoes might force a nail to grow back in. There might be poisoning in his system, blood rotting at the edges and flowing deep in congested waves.

He washed carefully and, when he shaved, his hand shook for fear he would cut his throat. He'd meant to get an electric razor. Why did he always forget? He looked in the cabinet. It was full of death. An unwary opening of bottles, a swallow and quick finish. He slammed the cabinet door shut and hurried out of the bathroom.

He descended slowly on the stairs so he wouldn't fall and shatter his body at the foot of the steps. His house was a trap, a snare set by himself and all the men and women who made it what it was. Shifting rugs and loose connections. Smooth floors and smoother bathtubs, burning radiators and fireplaces and furnaces. Broken glass and razor blades and splinters and sharp knives. Man built himself a home and filled it with menace. It was all right when you didn't think about it. But then something happened and you thought about it all the time.

At breakfast he wondered if maybe Lucy was poisoning him. She loved him. He knew that. She had married him and borne him two fine children. But maybe she was poisoning him. Maybe there was poison in the orange juice, sprinkled in with the salt and pepper and the sugar. Maybe he was packing death into his veins shouting — Here! Run riot in my blood!

He shuddered when she brushed against him. He was afraid for the children. And he was afraid of the children. They were his. He loved them with all his heart. He was afraid of them. Breakfast and supper on weekdays were agonies of wretched ambivalence. It got so he hated everyone at some time or another.

The subway station was very crowded. There were people lined up at the edge of the platform. The train whistled far away. They all shifted on their feet and moved closer to the edge. They touched him, pushed him, shoved him. He wanted to scream. They were trying to push him over the edge.

Suppose they did. Suppose the great steel mass slammed into him and crushed him to a pulp on the track, severed his limbs from his body, sent sprays of his blood into the air, splattered his organs on the black ties, coated the pillars with his flesh.

He wanted to yell, to strike out blindly, to fight for his life. But he was civilized. He was a modern.

He was a man. He couldn't cry or shriek. He had to pretend he wasn't afraid. He must make believe he was used to this — the surrounding of death in life.

The train was crowded. It was always crowded in the morning. The sweat trickled down his face and across his neck and down from his armpits. The people were packed against him. Packed people were death. Alone they were bad enough. In a mass, in a swaying dimlit mass, they were death itself. They mingled with each other, each of them joined with another and, all added up, they were crawling twisting death, all around him. Calling him, plucking at his clothes with flesh-tattered skeleton fingers.

He wondered if he should get off and take the local because there were always less people on the local.

But it was figuring like that that killed a man. Suppose he got on the local in order to avoid the crowds on the express. That day the local would have an accident. He knew it would. That was the way.

Then again, the local went under the river and the express went over it. If he was going to face death then he would rather it was on the express than on the local. Because it would be better to fall off the bridge. There might be a chance — just an outside chance — that he could get to a window and maybe swim up to the surface. He could see the light anyway. It would be better to see the light.

If there was an accident under the river he couldn't see anything. It would be pitch black. If the tunnel walls collapsed and the water rushed in, he'd be drowned in muddy torrential darkness. It would be dark because the electricity would short circuit. There would be people electrocuted and screaming and in the dark he could smell their flesh burning. He couldn't stand that. Water rushing up, up, swimming over him, screams in the blackness and drowning. Floating corpses in the black tunnel filled with water. It would be better to go the other way.

He took the express. And the people pushed against him and the train got more crowded at every station. He couldn't bear to be touched by the people. He shrank away from them and tried to stand apart. How did he know that some of them didn't have awful diseases and if they touched him he might get the disease too. Heat made germs float around in the air. Invisible little bugs floating on coughs and everybody's breath.

He had to get away. There had to be somewhere. Everywhere he went there was death and

he was afraid. He wanted to live. But death was everywhere. He couldn't get away from it.

At the office, he shivered at his desk. Suppose the building caught on fire and he was trapped. The flames roaring around and blisters and reddening skin and burning alive, horror stricken screams. He couldn't bear such agony.

Suppose the building collapsed. He'd heard of such things happening. After all, he was placing his life in the hands of an architect and engineers and builders and how did he know they were trustworthy? How did he know some engineer wasn't mad at something and he didn't make the right figures and seams cracked and the building caved in. The huge beams would crush him. He'd be hurtled to the sidewalk. His head would pop on the concrete like an egg and his brains would spill all over the sidewalk.

He thought about these things all the time. He couldn't work. He sat and scribbled on pieces of paper and thought about dying. How could a man concentrate when he was always fearing? He wanted to live but he couldn't see how. Everything was against him. There weren't any percentages. Everywhere he went death was waiting for him. He had nothing to say about it. It was going to happen and maybe in the next second. He couldn't alter it. All he could do was think and wonder about it and drive himself sick with worrying.

At lunch he thought that the waiter and the cook in the restaurant were conspiring to poison him. He couldn't eat the food. It choked in his throat. He ate little bits of it to see if he could taste any poison. He tried to dilute it with water.

Then he broke out into a cold sweat because it occurred to him that the water might be poisoned too. So he made the waiter bring him some water from the next table. He knew he was a fool for trying to trick the waiter. But he had to do it anyway.

All afternoon he wanted to scream and leap up from his desk and crash through the window. But he was afraid. He couldn't jump. He couldn't cry out — For God's sake, leave me be! He sat at his desk and shook with palsied terror. His brain teemed with many thoughts of the many ways a man can die each day. Each was more terrible than the one before. Each heaped its horror on the next until, after a while, he was no better than a helpless child whimpering in the night, fearing each sudden sound and movement. He hungered for peace and there was no peace. Terror was his only food.

When work ended at five, he had to go back to the subway. By that time he was gutted with horror and he stood dull-eyed and limp and was too weak to even shudder. Once more he went through the whole train of thought about the local and the express. It was like a separate litany in his brain. He couldn't stop it any more than he could voluntarily stop breathing.

At home he found the same threats waiting for him. He unlocked the door and stepped into the trap he had formed around him. He ate supper, hating and distrusting his wife and his children and even himself. Fear surrounded him like a shifting mist.

He was afraid of the house. He was more afraid to leave it. Lucy complained. But he wouldn't go anywhere. He sat in his chair quietly and clung to the arms and tried to keep from screaming. Then his mind began to pick out sounds and he began to feel death walking in his house, watching and waiting for him to make one slip, one incautious move.

He wanted to live!

He wanted to live in peace and quiet but they wouldn't let him.

He went to bed early because there was no comfort in waking. He tossed and turned alone. Lucy would not go to bed so early. She stayed downstairs and read.

He tried to think of nothing. But his mind would not blank itself. It went on and on. The roof was cracking, the floor was giving, the house was on fire, his system ran with poison, he was sick with infesting germs, there was a prowler with a gun, there was a mad dog outside the door, Lucy was sneaking up the stairs with a butcher knife.

He turned and screamed into the pillow so no one could hear his madness ringing out in the night.

Later he drifted away.

He dreamed the same dream over and over. The falling object, the ugly mushroom of billowing smoke, the spray of burning fire. He writhed with agony as it covered him. There were people watching. Lucy — he screamed — Lucy kill me, please kill me. I can't bear the pain. Please, please kill me.

She laughed at him. His children laughed. Everyone passed him by and laughed.

He was in torture. His body flared up. It was a white hot coal. He screamed from the pain. But they made him live. Live, live! — they cried. It was a chant in the night, a taunt from the blackness of dreaming. Death would not come then and take away the pain. It stood and watched but would not come close.

He cried, he screamed and woke up to find himself sitting in bed and staring at the night.

The same nightmare? — said Lucy.

Yes — he said.

He sat up for an hour. Then he fell back in a stupor of weariness. He closed his eyes and prayed for a dreamless rest.

And in the early morning when he had just about managed to fall into a troubled sleep — Lucy woke him up.

🕷

Stephen King and Dean Koontz have paid due and proper homage to Richard Matheson, who is the acknowledged American master of horrific fiction . . . though Matheson, who dislikes the breakdown of literature into genres, insists that a good story is a work of art, period. Born in 1926 in New Jersey, Matheson has written such classics as "Born of Man and Woman," "Dress of White Silk," I Am Legend, The (Incredible) Shrinking Man, *and the ultimate haunted-house novel,* Hell House. *He has written many TV and film screenplays, notable among them Steven Spielberg's first film,* Duel, *as well as* The Night Stalker, Twilight Zone's *"Nightmare at 20,000 Feet," and in collaboration with the late Charles Beaumont,* Burn Witch Burn, *the cinematic version of Fritz Leiber's* Conjure Wife.

Matheson, who has also written excellent western novels, has won the Bram Stoker Life Achievement Award, the Edgar, the Hugo, and the World Fantasy Life Achievement Award.

MATHESON'S MOVIES: A CRITICAL OVERVIEW

by Michael McCarty

Richard Matheson's name is synonymous with classic creepy cinema and television (including many masterpieces for *The Twilight Zone* and for TV movies produced by Dan Curtis, *The Night Stalker, Trilogy Of Terror,* as well as the early Steven Spielberg vehicle *Duel*). Matheson has written a number of screenplays. Many of his novels were adapted for the silver screen and TV. Here are some of his best motion-picture work:

The Incredible Shrinking Man (1957). Just a year after the publication of *The Shrinking Man,* Matheson wrote the screenplay from his own book. A very literate script that turned the giant-monster movies of the 1950s (*The Amazing Colossal Man, Attack of the 50-Foot Woman* and numerous behemoth bug flicks) on their heads. Scott Carey (played by Grant Williams) is a victim of the effects of silvery flakes of atomic radiation. As he begins to shrink smaller and smaller his new size means that everyday objects take on sinister meaning and he must fight for his life in an increasingly hostile and taller world. This movie was directed by Jack Arnold (who did such great genre films as *It Came From Outer Space, Tarantula,* and *Creature From The Black Lagoon* with special effects by Clifford Stine) and is a philosophical thriller and sci-fi classic.

The Last Man On Earth (1964). This is the first adaptation of *I Am Legend* (but without the use of Matheson's own screenplay). Hammer Films originally purchased the rights to the novel and hired the author to work on the screenplay. However, the British censor's office let it be known that the movie would be banned in England and Hammer stopped filming. Besides Bram Stoker's *Dracula,* or Anne Rice's *Interview With A Vampire,* Matheson's novella *I Am Legend,* is one of the most intriguing, imaginative, and influential vampire stories ever written. George Romero's *Night Of The Living Dead* was inspired by this book.

Vincent Price is the sole survivor of a mysterious plague that has turned the rest of the planet's population into vampires. After the sun sets, he barricades himself against the bloodsuckers that surround his home. During the day he gathers garlic, makes stakes, and destroys vampires.

Price was perfect for the rôle. I especially enjoy the scenes with him playing loud jazz music and drinking plenty of alcohol to drown out the noise of the vampires trying to break in. His past, however, still plagues him.

A creepy and atmospheric thriller despite its low budget. One of the eeriest moments occurs when Price is driving along streets that are cluttered with dead bodies.

In 1971, the film was remade with a bigger budget and in color as *The Omega Man* with Charlton Heston. But that movie was even further away from Matheson's material, and the vampiric elements were watered down. A third remake was in the works. It was to be called *I Am Legend* and to be directed by Ridley Scott. It was to star Arnold Schwarzenegger but went over-budget and folded. Rumors are now circulating that Will Smith will be in a film version of *I Am Legend.*

The Last Man On Earth is recommended, but more recommended is reading Matheson's book. The book's influence is still felt today in films like *28 Days Later.*

The Legend Of Hell House (1975). A multi-millionaire hires a team of scientists and mediums to investigate his newly-acquired haunted mansion. The creepy house has been the site of several deaths and may hold clues to the afterlife. Pamela Franklin, Roddy McDowall, Clive Revill, and Gayle Hunnicutt roam the dire dwelling and battle various manifestations (some great special effects by Roy Whybrow) emanating from the corpse of the late homeowner. Matheson wrote the screenplay from his novel *Hell House,* a suspenseful and scary screamfest.

Somewhere In Time (1980). Christopher Reeves plays a playwright (in his first post-Clark Kent rôle) who falls in love with a beautiful woman in an old portrait (of the lovely Jane Seymour). Through self-hypnosis he goes back in time to 1912 to discover what their relationship might have been. A romantic science-fiction tearjerker that made a star of the Grand Hotel on Mackinac Island in Lake Michigan, where the film was shot. Based on Matheson's *A Bid In Time.*

What Dreams May Come (1998). Robin Williams does a brilliant job this dazzling special-effects-laden fantasy about how love can survive death and how Heaven and Hell can't stop true romance. Cuba Gooding, Jr., also does a remarkable job in his supporting rôle. The special effects are mind blowing, sometimes overshadowing this classic story. The title is a Shakespeare reference. Overall, worth checking out.

Stir of Echoes (1999). Kevin Bacon plays a blue-collar man in Chicago. After being hypnotized at a neighborhood party, he sees things he can't explain and hears voices he can't ignore. Echoes of a past crime haunt his mind. He plunges into a shattering encounter with a dead girl, and his world is never the same again.

The film was eclipsed by the success of *The Sixth Sense*, which was released at about the same time. *Stir of Echoes* is the creepier of the two.

It is a chilling classic based on Matheson's novel, *A Stir of Echoes*. ✿

ONE DAY AT A TIME

by Charles Black

The trail was rocky, littered with boulders. Two men rode that way, heading towards the town of Abilene. I knew them both.

My sudden appearance spooked their horses. The riders struggled to bring their steeds under control. One of them, Clay Johnson, was able to rein in his rearing mount, but his companion was not so fortunate, or so skilful a horseman.

He could not curb his panicked steed, and he was thrown from the saddle. He cracked his skull on a jagged rock. Death was instantaneous; I did not need to check. I knew Pete Day was dead.

Which was fine, I did not want Clay's life; indeed, I wanted a witness to tell what he had seen.

"My God, it can't be you!" he exclaimed.

I made sure he got a good look at me. "It's me, Clay; you can believe it; and you make sure you tell Pete's brothers too."

*   *   *

I found Jake Day cowering in a clapboard church; the nervous one of the three, he knew with mounting fear that I would be coming for him. When I found him he was on his knees, praying to his God for salvation. With trembling hands he held a wooden crucifix before him. I brushed it aside, saying, "That won't do, you no good son, I aint no vampire."

My grin was a fixed rictus as, shivering and shaking with fear, he begged me for his life. Then his features were marred by a sudden grimace of pain, and he cried out, clasping his chest. Jake Day was having a fatal heart attack.

*   *   *

Clem Day was last. He was drinking whiskey in a saloon in Dodge. I called him out.

Tumbleweeds rolled along the dusty street, and someone ran to fetch the sheriff.

"So it is true, it is you. I thought that fool Clay was addled when he told me about Pete. Well, I be damned."

"Oh you're damned a'right, Clem," I said.

Clem sneered, "Bullets took care of you before, they can do so again."

I noticed that the sheriff had arrived just in time to hear Clem's confession.

"Not even silver bullets will help you this time Clem," I said.

He drew and fired in the blink of an eye. He'd always been fast, not that it mattered — as I said, his bullets couldn't hurt me again — but he kept on firing.

His expression of sneering arrogance was replaced by one of shocked disbelief as I kept on coming. And I wrapped my bony fingers around Clem's throat and squeezed that life out of him.

Now I, Edgar Day, cunning man, and father of three no-good sons, am avenged and can rest in peace. ✿

MY! WHAT BIG TEETH THEY HAVE

by Melissa Kirkwood Lewis

She giggled, her long braid swinging as she scampered up the monkey bars. A gibbous moon watched, the churning clouds masking its partially transformed face. It was less than a week to maturity.

She crossed a single rung at a time. She bent her knees stiffly as if to keep her new pink tennis shoes from being tainted by the mud puddles in the worn track beneath. She reached the end and dismounted with a clumsy backward somersault.

"Hello."

She jumped. She panted through her slightly parted lips as she looked in the direction of the voice. A figure approached. A man.

"Hello," he said again.

He stood about four feet from her now. He stopped.

"Doesn't your mommy know you're out here? Most little girls are in bed by now."

"You're not going to tell Mommy, are you?"

"Nah. Listen, I was walking my dog, Sparky, and he got away. See, I still have his leash. You haven't seen him, have you? A little brown puppy about this high?"

"I thought I heard a doggie a few minutes ago."

"Where, sweetheart?"

She pointed to the deep shadows where the tall, dense hedges grew.

"You are the sweetest little girl I ever met. And the prettiest. Can you take me over there and show me?"

She shyly took his sweating hand and together they walked to the hedges. She pushed her way through and he followed, fingering the leash in his spare hand.

Screaming. Begging. A dreadful ripping and crunching.

After a while, the little girl emerged from the bushes, wiping her mouth on the back of her hand.

"So?"

"You were right, Mommy. It was easy."

"And the scraps?"

"Ground up and buried."

"Very good."

She embraced the child, cleaning blood from her cheek and chin.

"I'm so proud of you."

She took her child's hand.

"Now it's Mommy's turn."

And together they flew off into the night.   🕷

Melissa Lewis lives in Zachary, LA, with her husband Chris, three blocks from the playground in the story.
This is her second publication.

THE DARK

by R.J. Lewis

illustrated by Britt Spencer

Jake Hurd never got used to the dark. Actually, it wasn't darkness as much as the things that were hiding in it.

That's why I became involved. I am a licensed psychiatrist in the great state of New Jersey. I deal with the crazies, the misfits, the insecure, and of course, the people who see things.

When I was called in on the case, I thought it was no big deal. Human beings are afraid of the dark. It's a common primeval fear that strikes us as children. As adults, we try not to let it overpower our egos, until we find ourselves someplace dark and unsafe, at which point most of us become the frightened prey of our prehistoric past.

The man who called me in on the case, Dr. Bill Benning, is an old friend and a good golf partner. He told me I would have to keep the case very hush-hush. The patient was a security guard, and this old fellow was some kind of poster boy for guards. Now that's an image!

The security company wanted us to keep his head screwed on until he reached retirement, about another five years.

So, agreeing to a fee higher than my usual, I felt I could give this case a high priority with low publicity. It would be easy. A man who spends his time walking through dim hallways alone has ample time to dream up nightmares. I decided some time on the couch, a few visualization exercises, and if necessary, an antidepressant or two and he would be fine.

Then I met Jake.

He must have been tall when he was younger — 6'5" or 6'6", but over the years his shoulders slouched. I really didn't expect a man fifty-nine years old who looked seventy-nine. Most of his hair was gone, leaving wisps of white at his temples and a flesh-colored dome on top.

He was being kept at the hospital for observation due to a suicide attempt.

I remember the day he walked into my office wearing his hospital gown and a robe. His legs bore scars from numerous cuts and gouges. Whatever he was doing to himself, the slashing of his wrists was not the first time he had cut himself. I invited him to sit down.

"So, Jake — can I call you Jake?"

"I don't mind," he said.

"I understand you've been having troubles, Jake."

"That's what they tell me," he answered.

"Do you want to talk about it?"

"That depends," he said, looking at me intently as if watching my every reaction. "Do you really want to know? I mean, the whole story?"

"Whatever you want to tell me," I said, smiling.

An odd smile crossed his lips, and he said, "Okay, but you did ask. It began forty years ago." And he began to tell me the story of his life.

Jake didn't plan to live in the night, walking through obscure hallways and lightless stairwells. In fact, when he was a young man, the idea of being a security guard struck him as a joke, something to do for a year or two.

As a therapist, I thought this was a healthy attitude. A lot of security guards want to be cops, and act like they are.

Jake started on his first assignment at the age of nineteen. He applied at the dirty, busy office from an ad he saw in a newspaper. The security company immediately offered him a position working midnight to eight in the morning. The company didn't train him, they just gave him a uniform, and sent him to the job site. His first night, another guard showed him the rounds.

Jake was fascinated by the watchclock, a large, heavy circular machine with a clock face and an oversized keyhole. He would walk throughout the unilluminated factory going from one place to another. At each point he would locate a large metal key chained to the wall. He would insert the key in the clock and move on.

That first night as the other guard walked him through the gloomy factory, Jake looked at the areas that seemed to be in permanent shadows.

He couldn't fight the odd feeling that there was something there. This instinct grew as he began to do the rounds by himself.

"Something?" I interrupted. "Can you be a little more specific?"

"Yes," Jake said nodding, "it was like eyes were watching my every move. It was as though the dark was aware of me."

I wrote a note on the pad of paper in my lap, and asked him to continue.

Jake said that he ignored the feeling, swallowed his fear, and did the rounds anyway. In fact, he did them deliberately, slowly. He began to want to try to get a glimpse of whatever it was hiding in the gloom. He would shine his flashlight into corners, suddenly. He would turn on light switches when he detected movement, trying to catch whatever was there in a sudden flood of light.

But whatever lived in the lightless areas was too quick, too clever. Jake would never catch them. But he knew they were there.

"That's all we have time for today," I said, "but I will see you tomorrow." Jake agreed, and an orderly took him back to his hospital room. I went about the rest of my day, but that night, I found I had trouble sleeping.

My next session with Jake, I was a bit tired and bleary eyed, but I pressed on.

"What did you do at night, on your rounds, when you felt these eyes watching you?" I asked.

"Thinking and — planning. There was time for both."

Jake went on, telling me that he stayed at that assignment until the factory closed ten years later. By now the security company had clean offices that were in a nice building, but he was moved to another factory just as bleak and uninteresting. The company liked him; he showed up on time, did his rounds with a diligence few others possessed. The company didn't know he was looking for the things in the shadows.

"That was thirty years ago," said Jake.

The new location, dull and depressing as the previous one, actually was a relief at first. For days, it appeared to him that the eyes weren't there. Jake felt calmer, relieved, as if maybe the whole thing had been in his mind. But in less than one week, he sensed them again. Sometimes just around a corner, sometimes watching him from above. Wherever there were shadows for them to hide.

At the new factory, there were some advantages. He met a secretary at the factory and talked to her every morning. Finally, he worked up the nerve and asked her out. Jake said she was about average height, with average looks, and average needs, but she was a little dynamo of energy. He found her positive and upbeat personality a refreshing change from the dreary thoughts that pervaded his own mind. They married, and a daughter was born less than a year after the wedding.

"I guess back then I was as happy as I've ever been," Jake said, with a look on his face that didn't suggest happiness.

The schedule of working nights meshed well with his wife's schedule of daytime work. A slight change in her arrival time, and they could both raise their child. She was home in the evening and at night. He was there during the day, and slept in the evening. The daughter flourished and grew, raised by either one parent or the other.

"I wish we'd had more than one," Jake said, "but my wife wouldn't hear of it."

But as the eyes watched Jake during the night, Jake began to find that they didn't stay at the factory, at work. He became aware that they were following him during the early evening, or sometimes even at home, in his darkened bedroom. He would be sleeping, and suddenly jump up and pull open the curtains with a yank to let the sunlight pour in, trying to catch the intruders. The behavior frightened his wife and his daughter.

"If they had just helped me!" Jake said.

"What would that have done?" I pointed out.

"Then maybe, just maybe, I would've caught them," Jake lamented.

That ended that session, and I wrote up my notes. This was going to be an interesting case after all. I began to think I could get a psychiatric paper out of Jake and his "things in the dark."

Unfortunately, I would eventually have to tell the security company things that they didn't want to hear: advanced paranoia, schizophrenia, possible delusions.

That night I didn't sleep much better. I left the light on in the bathroom, which was reassuring, but ultimately didn't help.

The next day, Jake told me that he began to make elaborate traps to catch them. He felt this way he could prove that the creatures were real. He tried to explain to his wife and little girl why these odd contrivances were important, and the need to be careful around them. His wife thought them a danger, and was getting more and more upset by Jake's behavior.

"I just wanted to protect us," he said, "to scare those things off, to get them to bother someone else."

He bought lights that were more powerful and brighter to try to fill every inch of the house with safe, white light. It was on one of those lamps that his little girl burned her hand. She accidentally tripped over a power cord and the heavy light, balanced on a three-legged stand, fell over on her. They needed to go to the hospital, where the doctor said the broken and burned hand would never be the same. The next day, his wife got a court order, and Jake couldn't go home any more. She also filed for divorce, for mental and emotional cruelty.

"That was twenty years ago," Jake said, "when the divorce became final."

Jake moved to a small apartment, the child support making it necessary to live simply. But he didn't really mind. It was smaller, easier to light, easier to build traps. It was during this time he became fixated on electronics.

His visitations with his daughter were limited. What's more, the court sided with his wife in ordering that he couldn't talk about the creatures. That he found difficult.

"I mean, how can she protect herself if she doesn't know what to look for?" Jake said, exasperated.

Ultimately Jake accepted it, decided it was for the best. After all, this way the things couldn't overhear him talking about a trap. That made it more possible for him to catch them unawares.

"You mean, the things might have overheard you talking about what measures you were taking?" I said, trying to understand.

"Of course, Doc," Jake said, as if it were obvious.

That was how that session ended, with Jake looking at me as if I was dense.

That night as I left a late night group therapy session, I had the strangest sensation as I walked to my car that I was being watched. I chortled to myself, at how Jake's stories were beginning to affect my perception. That night I slept in the guest room with the light on. I was finally able to sleep through the night.

In the next few sessions Jake told me the security company was bought by a larger outfit, who still kept Jake on. They kept moving him from location to location. He was now walking a shift where he carried keys, and a computer could track his locations where he would insert a key in a wall-mounted keyhole.

He didn't tell any of the changing array of coworkers about his interest, though he did show the supervisors some of the motion detectors he built. The company actually bought the rights to several of Jake's inventions, and gave him awards, credit, and a hefty percentage of the profits for some of the innovations. The equipment was cutting-edge and it was helping the company grow and prosper.

I realized why I was brought on the case in such a quiet way. The company didn't want the public to know that their innovator, the man behind some of their best security tools, was a raving paranoid.

Jake invented the machines to catch the things in the dark, and he figured if they were used by his company, he would have the chance to use them on a larger scale. But he found it was the same problem as when he changed locations. The devices would keep them away for a while, but sooner or later they would figure it out and return. In fact, once the things learned how a device worked, it wouldn't even hamper them. They could still watch Jake from the shadows.

"Then about ten years ago, I began to hear them," Jake said.

"Hear them?" I repeated as if I misunderstood.

"Well, I guess you'd say I became aware of their sounds."

Jake told me that it was small, voiceless sounds to begin with, rather like the wind passing through dry leaves. But as Jake began to listen more intently, he began to hear the creature's murmuring just beyond his consciousness.

"Were they saying anything?" I asked.

"No," Jake said, "just strange noises. Maybe they were talking to each other, but not to me. Their tones and frequencies seemed to be part of the background, but as I listened, I could tell they weren't."

Jake was still building his traps and alarms, and selling them to the company. His daughter was in college, and the money helped. He was making enough to buy a house — but he didn't.

His apartment was his bunker.

Being aware of their sounds, Jake possessed a new weapon in his arsenal. He tried to follow the creatures with not just his "feeling," but with his ears. As he continued to do his rounds, he would try to listen for them, so he could wait until they were close, turn on his flashlight, and hear them scurry away.

"I began to enjoy that," Jake said with a smile. "I would even sit some place dark, wait for them to come, and flip on the lights, so they had to flee."

"I guess you were frightening them for a change," I said.

"I guess," said Jake, swallowing hard.

"Tell me, Jake, you were a big success with your company. Why didn't you ask to be transferred to day shift?"

Jake looked at me like I was crazy.

"Yeah, they offered me a day job. Offered to make me head of a whole damn department." His voice dropped conspiratorially. "But I couldn't. I had to sleep in the daytime. When it was safe."

So this became Jake's life. Sleeping during the day, even on days he didn't work, then tinkering with devices in the early evening, and working midnight to eight at a security post. He now was a captain, and did more paperwork. But even so, he insisted on doing one round a night "to stay in shape."

"Wait a minute," I interjected, "was that the real reason?"

"Of course not," Jake said, "but that's what I had to tell them."

Jake, of course, was using the time to study the noises from the darkness. He wanted to keep his ear trained, so the sounds could be reproduced.

"I guess during this time I started to become less frightened of them. That was a mistake. I also figured a way to catch some of them, really catch them, not like the other times." Jake looked at his feet. "I guess that was a mistake, too."

"So, Jake, how did you think you could catch one of these things?"

"I made a detector," he said. "It was a beauty. A small, out-of-the-way sonic device that could be fine-tuned to almost any sound, even as faint as the wind." Jake smiled from the memory. "It could be attached to anything: an alarm, a phone, or even a powerful halogen light."

Jake went on to elaborate with excitement about these lights, very new then, that created an astounding amount of illumination very quickly.

He convinced the security company to let him run trials with the new lights.

He set up a large, open space in the factory where the entire area, several hundred square feet, would be filled with a dazzling light. Even with tests done during the day, the light output required Jake to wear protective goggles.

"When it was finally ready, I made a little remote control to turn on the detector. Then that night I waited until three, maybe four in the morning. I went to that section of the factory, sat in a chair, stock still," Jake told me.

He used a large, dark part of the warehouse, a storage area filled with display pieces that the factory put up at Christmas time. Big boxes of artificial trees and mechanical elves lay strewn in unnatural positions. He knew it was one of the creatures' favorite places.

He sat utterly still waiting for their noises, their little clickety-clacks and whispers in the dark. In the distance he could hear the background noises the water pumps and the air conditioning units made.

He was waiting . . . waiting for their undertones.

He waited, and then heard a very quiet tap that he recognized. He held still, his finger on the button that would activate his sonic apparatus.

Waiting, he could hear more — and more taps. He held his thumb at the ready, waiting for them to draw closer. Then he pushed the button and tried to breathe as lightly as he could, trying not to make even the faintest sound.

He could feel them all around him, hovering in the shadows, in the dark. He could hear them making their little noises, the ones he tried so hard to adjust his sonic equipment to detect.

Would the detector hear those faint whispers or was it all in his mind?

The lights shot on with a dazzling impact. Jake was wearing his special goggles, protecting his eyes from the blinding illumination.

"That's when I saw them," he said.

"You saw them?"

"Yes, in the light, with no place to run and no

shadows to hide in. For a moment, I could see them."

I was stunned. This was entirely against standard paranoid behavior. I was afraid Jake might be severely delusional. I asked him, "What did these — things look like?"

"Like shadows," Jake said. "They were flat, two dimensional beasts with square heads and jagged lines that were their eyes and mouths. They looked at me, angry, and then they were gone, they ran away so fast to hide in the darkness, somewhere else."

After that session I started looking through my Physicians Desk Reference to try to find a drug that would help with a case where the patient appeared rational but as far gone as Jake was. It would've been easier if I didn't keep needing to adjust the lights. The shadows in my room seemed very — close.

In the next sessions, Jake told me he tried to trap them again, this time with a special camera to record them. But the creatures didn't take the bait. They knew where he set up the lights, and wouldn't return for days. The days stretched into weeks.

"It was kind of nice," Jake said. "I actually slept a couple of nights, and visited my grandchild one day. My daughter had a little girl around that time, and I finally got a chance to see her."

Jake thought the creatures were gone. But he was wrong.

When they came back, a few weeks later, it was different. They were no longer content to watch him from the dark. They were angry.

"That was five years ago," Jake said, "they were different, more aggressive."

At first, when Jake was aware they were back, it was the same as it had been, watching him. But now sometimes in the darkness he felt them touch him. At first it was fleetingly, like a butterfly passing over his skin. But he knew these touches were not friendly. In fact, the first time it happened, Jake was nearly scared to death.

Then it escalated. Small touches became bigger, more often, more to let Jake know who was in charge.

Then one night, Jake did his round, which was on a post that required a walk through the machine shop. Jake no longer wore a uniform like a police officer; he now wore a brown suit that matched all the other guards. More corporate, less cop. He was carrying a device called a Morse gun, designed to fit little plastic rectangles situ-

ated all over the factory. His route was timed and tracked by a computer chip in the gun, and he always had five minutes to get to the next key.

So, as Jake walked into the machine shop, he knew they were there, hiding in all the shadows. They always did. But the noises — they weren't trying to hide at all, he could hear them. He walked by the different lathes, wood working, and metal cutting machines, all silent in the night.

Something grabbed his leg, hard!

Jake fell forward, smacking into a machine. He fell to the floor, his head bleeding profusely.

"That's how I got this," Jake said, pointing to the scar on his head. Jake showed me the scars on his legs and arms. I assumed before that it was a symptom of his mental state. Self mutilation is not uncommon for a delusional patient.

Jake grabbed for his flashlight, getting back up to his feet. He shone the bright light wildly, trying to chase them away. He thought he saw one move through the beam, and Jake pursued it toward a large sheet metal cutter in the corner of the room.

Jake kept catching glimpses of it, then he heard the big machine power up.

"They could actually turn on switches," Jake said excitedly. "I went to turn it off — that's when they tripped me."

"Tripped you?" I said.

"Clean pulled my legs out from under me," Jake said. He fell to the ground and tried to pull himself up.

"But something, one of them, was pulling on my hand."

Jake looked up to see his hand right under the huge cutting blade.

"I turned and rolled, pulling my hand out just as that blade came down," Jake said. Just remembering was making him sweat. "I got up unsteadily to my feet. But all around me, the machines started turning on." His eyes glazed over as the memory took him. "I ran out of the building, outside into the night air, but they kept tripping me. I had to use my radio to call for help."

His fellow officers found him outside the machine-shop building, covered with mud and babbling incoherently. He went to the hospital and got five stitches in his head.

"How did you explain this to the other guards?" I asked.

"That was easy," Jake chuckled. "I told them I slipped in some oil, fell, and hit my head. Hitting my head caused me to talk incoherently and fall in the mud."

A logical answer.

"So, once again, you hid your obsession from others," I said.

"I didn't want them to think I was crazy," Jake said. "After all, you think I'm crazy."

I sighed. This was a normal moment in therapy, but the one I always dreaded.

"Well, Jake, you did try to take your own life."

Jake moved closer to me and spoke quietly and intently. "That's what they want you to think, Doctor. The last few years have been Hell. They kept doing things to me, not as big as the machine shop, but little things. Metal pieces moved into my path, knives, whatever they could get." He held up his wrists to show me the bandages. "They did this."

I quieted my tone to match his. "Okay, Jake. How did they do that?"

Jake sat back and inhaled deeply.

Jake told me he had grown tired of the endless pokes and bumps they did to him during the night. So he planned to end it. He built another little device. A small strobe, no bigger than a camera flash, that could oscillate like a disco light, but much, much brighter. It had taken years, and Jake had to outfit himself with a large battery pack, constructed like a vest under his clothes. The strobe itself was two small units he wore clipped on his belt under his jacket. All he would have to do is pull up his jacket and activate the strobes.

"And this time," Jake said, "I built a camera. A small one that I put in the belt buckle to take pictures while the strobes flashed. I figured then I'd have proof! Then people would have to believe me, and help me get rid of them."

That night, wearing his special vest and belt, Jake took an early post — around midnight, and began to walk it. He could hear them, angry and grumbling in their whispering way.

He jumped. One touched his leg.

Too soon — too soon — got to get them bolder.

"Come on, you cowards," Jake remembered saying. He moved to the part of the factory where there was open space. He walked into the cafeteria, which was big, open, and had very few lights on.

He could hear them, feel them, they were grabbing at his legs, and rubbing his bald head.

"This is it!" Jake yelled, pulling the jacket out of the way and activating the strobes.

It was the first time he heard the things scream.

The lights flashed repeatedly, freezing the dark shapes in the flashing light. But it was different from the other time. The strobe light gave them depth, made them look three dimensional. They covered the slits of their eyes with their stunted limbs as they howled.

Jake roared as his little camera clicked away. "There you go — *bastards!*" he yelled. This was it! He finally had his victory. That's when one of the little things grabbed a chair and shoved it against him. Then another hit him with a trash can. The others grabbed whatever they could and hit him, threw things at him.

"The connections to the strobes were far too delicate," Jake said. "They tore them loose, and then they all pounced on me in the darkness."

As Jake told it, they threw him to the floor, smashed his lights, and then one of them came in with a huge knife from the kitchen.

Jake hit the button on his radio, yelling for help, but the creatures pulled his hands up, and the one with the knife neatly slit his wrists. As the blood poured down his arms, Jake blacked out, listening to the sound of his own screaming.

"I woke up here in the hospital, and that's when you and I started to talk."

I put my pen down. "Jake. . . ." I said simply.

"It's all true," Jake said. "Read my medical report when I came in. There was bruising along my hips from impact with heavy objects."

"Jake," I said, "you could have slit your own wrists and fallen against something. You're asking me to believe a lot without any proof."

Jake moved closer, whispering in my ear. "I've got the photos from my little camera."

"Jake, are you sure you didn't imagine this?"

"No, no," Jake said, whispering again. "But you should come to my room before nightfall. I'll give you the film. You can get it developed — then you'll have your proof."

I said I would, and Jake was taken back to his room.

I sat at my desk for a while just going over my notes. This case was more than a psychiatric paper. Hell, Jake could be a book, even possibly a

life's work.

I met with other patients, but for me it was a halfhearted effort, listening to them whine about their mothers. As soon as my patients were done for the day, I sat at my computer and transcribed my notes about Jake. I didn't really keep track of time, until I looked up from my screen and saw it was ten o'clock.

I realized I was supposed to meet Jake, but it was way after hours. Even so, it wasn't a good choice to leave someone who is afraid of the dark waiting at night. I saved my work, and started to walk to Jake's room.

It was ghostly, walking the hallways at night. The corridors always seemed so busy and full of life during the day. Now, the lights were turned down, and I could walk down hallways that were dark from end to end.

I turned. What did I hear? A sound, so quiet, yet so out of place. Of course, it was nothing, it had to be. I was letting Jake's story and my imagination run wild.

I reached the main desk where the night nurse was on duty. Signing in, she told me the number of Jake's room. I walked down the hall, past the darkened rooms looking for Jake's. It should be easy to find, since he asked that the light always be on. In fact, I made sure to put the request on his chart.

I looked for the room with a light on, but I didn't see one. Checking the room numbers and realized I walked right past it. I began to retrace my steps, reading the numbers on each door as I went back. I reached Jake's door, and it was ajar, but the light in the room was off. Some new orderly didn't read his chart and turned it off. I knocked on the door and pushed it a little more open.

"Jake?" I said.

No reply. He was probably sedated, and I'd have to wait for this film of his tomorrow. I decided to turn the light on, in case he woke up in the night and panicked.

I stared into the darkness and flipped the light switch, causing the fluorescent light to flash and blink. I saw something in the darkness for a moment.

It only lasted for the time the light flickered and strobed, but I saw it. About three feet high, a dark mass, like a shadow, with slits for eyes and a jagged line for a mouth. It looked at me and hissed, like a cat.

I yelled out. As the lights came on full, it was gone.

It was standing near the bed, and now I could see Jake. He was sprawled on the bed, his head in an unnatural position, hanging off the side. The sheet was wrapped tightly around his neck. On his chest was a small thing, like a belt buckle, and a small roll of a thin film, laid out and exposed to the light, ripped and ruined.

My cry brought nurses and orderlies running. They ran past me and moved to Jake, seeing if he could be saved. I couldn't move. The image of the short dark thing embedded in my mind.

*   *   *

"So that's how Jake died?" Dr. Benning said. "He was killed by these creatures from his mind?"

"No, Doctor," I said, "the creatures were real."

Dr. Benning rubbed his chin. Then he looked at his watch and said, "Look, old boy, Jake died by falling out of his bed with a sheet wrapped around his neck. It was an accident."

I sighed and muttered, "It doesn't matter what you think. You have to protect me. Now they're after me, because I've seen one of them."

Dr. Benning looked at me and shook his head. "I'm afraid that's all the time for this session. The orderly will take you back to your room. Please don't fight the nurses, take your medication."

"Only if you give me the hand held button I asked for to turn on the lights in my room," I said.

"It's highly unusual, but I'll make sure they hook something up for you."

The orderly came in and escorted me back to my room. The nurses wandered around outside my room mumbling under their breaths about "the strain," and "poor fellow just went."

I don't care what they think. In the night, with the light on in my room, I sit and watch for them, always on my guard. I can hear them, just beyond the bright safety of my light, scratching and tapping. I know they're waiting to catch me, waiting for me —

In the dark.   1

✍   *Magician, entertainer, and author, R.J. Lewis has experienced every level of show business from street-performing to Broadway. He's happily married to his wife, Debra, and has one daughter, Rayna.*

His first job was working as a night guard, which started his vivid imagination turning toward the macabre.

A GHOST CAN BE BORN

by Ray Russell

At one in the morning, when Clayton Horne let himself into his Beverly Hills house and snapped on the lights, Chet Montague was sitting in the big orange chair. Nothing new in that — Chet was in the habit of appropriating the armchair for himself when he dropped in — but Horne was startled to see him. Before he could express his astonishment, Chet smiled his little half-smile and said, "Hi, pal."

Horne stood perplexed and pleased. "Chet! What the hell!"

Chet chuckled softly and comfortably. "You just going to stand there?"

Horne stepped further into the living room. "How long have you been sitting in the dark? How did you get in?"

Chet winked slyly. "Oh, I have ways."

"My god," Horne said with a sudden laugh, "it's good to see you, Chet!"

"Good to see you, pal."

"And you're looking great, just great." That was true: clad crisply, shaven to a pink glow, hair trimmed and brushed, eyes alert, Chet certainly did look great.

"Feel great," he said. "But *you* look terrible."

"Well, it's a shock, damn it, coming into a presumably empty house and . . . I could use a drink." Horne turned quickly toward the liquor table. "Join me?"

"No, thanks, but you go ahead."

Horne, his back to Chet, clawed the seal from a new bottle of Cutty Sark and splashed himself a massive jolt which he flung down his throat in one quick flicker of movement. He squeezed his eyes shut and let the whisky's small hard seed of power open up, blossom, shine sunnily in his stomach. During this, Chet was silent. Horne wondered why. He wondered if, when he opened his eyes and turned around, Chet would be gone.

No — he was still there, drumming his long fingers on the arm of the orange chair, smiling easefully at Horne. Through the picture window, Horne saw the bloated moon try to hide its lardy nakedness behind a cloud.

"Long time no see," Chet said.

"Too long. Much too long. How are you? I mean really: how do you feel?"

"I said. Great."

Horne could only grin sheepishly and scratch his head. At length, he admitted, "I can't get over it. It's so damned good to see you. What the hell are you doing here?"

Chet shrugged. "Just felt like a friendly chat. Of course, it *is* late. If you want to get to bed — "

"No! No, no, no. Stay right where you are. Don't budge. Just give me a minute to . . ."

"Adjust?" Chet chuckled. "Gave you a turn, didn't I?"

"It's just the suddenness. Sure you don't want a drink?"

"Some other time." Chet leaned back and propped up his long legs on the orange hassock. He sighed luxuriously. Then he said, "I had a dream within a dream the other night. Ever have that?"

"Never."

"I dreamt I was in my analyst's office — "

"You don't have an analyst."

"I know that! It's a *dream.* I was in his office, recounting a dream I'd had the night before. I was saying: 'You know that little club on La Cienega called The Losers? No? Well, they have a kind of marquee out front where they put up a new name every seven days. Loser of the Week, they call it. For instance, back when Liz started up with Burton, the name on the marquee was **Eddie Fisher**. Or, when the Baldwin Hills reservoir burst and we had that flood, the Loser of the Week was the Department of Water. And when the Surgeon General finally published that report on cigarettes and cancer it just said, **Smokers**. Anyway, I'm driving up La Cienega, past the club, and I turn to look at the sign, and it's my name. **Chet Montague**, it says, Loser of the Week. And everybody on the street turns and they all see me and they point and whisper and laugh. Then I wake up.'

"My analyst says, 'You told me that one Tuesday.'

" 'Well, I can't help it,' I tell him, 'it recurs.'

" 'Don't you have anything new?' he wants to know.

"I get mad: 'What, you're bored with the old ones? I have to keep you entertained? Who's paying who here?'

"He says, 'That's a very interesting reaction.' Then I wake up. I mean *really* wake up."

"Fascinating."

"I think so. Like the Pet Milk can within the can within the can within . . .'"

The hours zipped by, Horne drank steadily, and artistic disagreements developed, and obligatory insults were exchanged, and mutual pomposities were paraded, and it was enjoyable, stimulating, just like old times.

"Selby says he learned how to write by listening to Beethoven," Chet said at one point. "Extending the musical analogy —"

"Beethoven!" drunkenly snorted Horne.

"Extending the musical analogy," Chet patiently repeated, "I am the Rossini of writing."

"Don't tell me. Let me guess." Rising slowly, like a leviathan from the deep, Horne forsook his supine position on the couch and gravitated toward the depleted bottle of scotch which he purposely placed out of easy reach. Having made it to the bottle, he immediately about-faced and wended his way back to the couch, retrieved his glass, and set out for the bottle again, saying, during his trek, "Gioacchino Rossini, the composer, retired at the age of thirty-seven. You intend to do the same. Which would be like next year. Is that your message, Chet?"

"No." Chet doggedly explained: "It's been said of Rossini that he had the gifts of a genius and the soul of a hack. So I, me, your friend Chesley B. Montague, am the Rossini of writing. *Capish?*"

"Chet, you kill me."

"How come?"

Horne tilted the bottle, allowing a portion of scotch to fall out, most of which landed in his glass. He reached into the ice bucket, found only coolish water therein, and flicked his wet fingertips into his glass in a token gesture of dilution. "I'll tell you how come . . ."

But when he turned to face Chet, he found his friend had vanished. Not walked out on his legs, with corporeal footsteps and the opening and slamming of doors, but vanished. Disappeared.

"It figures," Horne mumbled to himself, looking blearily about the empty room. "It figures." He had been expecting it to happen at any moment. It had taken a long time — over two hours — but

Chet finally had been switched off, zap, just like that. Like a TV set.

Horne marched with rigid precision toward the bathroom, wobbling only slightly. He took off all his clothes, leaving them in a heap on the tile floor, and stepped into the shower stall. He turned on only the cold water, full force. He stood gasping under the barrage of frigid spikes, stood there until the icy water illusively seemed warm, then he turned it off and stepped dripping from the stall. As he dried his glistening body with a big fluffy towel, he thought about the visit from Chet:

Subjective, of course. Had to be. A full-scale, life-size, two-hour, 3-D pink elephant, wired for sound. An audio-visual hallucination, induced by wishful thinking.

But Horne had never before been subject to hallucinations. Not ever, not once. Well, he told himself, there's a first time for everything. You've finally flipped. Next stop, the rubber room. It was the only explanation.

Or was it? Horne stretched out naked on the bed, staring at the ceiling. The bedspread felt coarse to his bare skin. Was it really the only explanation? There was a touch of the mystic about Horne — a mere marbling, veined delicately through his otherwise solidly literal psyche — and it now compelled him to ask: or was it a ghost?

The ghost of Chet Montague who sat in the living room for two hours, talking, laughing, arguing. Was that it?

Don't be silly, Horne chided himself, swinging his feet to the floor and rising. He paced in the moon-blue bedroom, still naked. Don't be silly. How could it have been Chet's ghost?

That's impossible. Not that ghosts are impossible, necessarily. Manifestations of persistent personal energy, scientifically explicable, telepathic in nature, continuing after the shock of death. Paranatural, not supernatural. Horne did not "believe in" ghosts; neither did he disbelieve in them. Still, in regard to a ghost of Chet Montague, he again told himself don't be silly. Whatever he had seen tonight, it couldn't have been Chet's ghost, and for a very good reason, the best reason in the world:

Chet wasn't dead.

Unless suddenly tonight — no, a quick phone call to the night desk at The Home confirmed that Chet was alive.

He felt chilly. He wrapped a robe around his gooseflesh, slid his feet into cruelly cold slippers, and walked to the kitchen, where he set about brewing a pot of coffee . . .

The horror had begun slowly, he recalled as he waited for the coffee to boil. It had crept upon Chet imperceptibly at first, with stealth, with subtlety. An infinitesimal loss of color in his work, a loss unnoticed by many, a widening but indefinable dearth. Later, an increasing reliance upon researchers, then collaborators, finally ghostwriters to whose labors he would add very little, then virtually nothing, then nothing. 'Writer's block,' his intimates said, shaking their heads.

Somewhere along the line, the heavy drinking had started, and was blamed for the fading of his powers. It was no cause, they now knew, but an effect, the refuge of a frightened, puzzled man to whom Something was happening, Something intangible without a name.

(It had a name, they later learned: a hyphenated, German-sounding name for a thing lacking both known cause and cure.)

Speech was the next to slow down, to become ponderous and deliberate, each word spotlighted, each phrase a major production. The personality became stilted and arid, as spontaneity and flexibility fled. And still the drink was blamed; and Chet was scorned and scoffed at, written off: here comes the old sponge again, El Lusho, He Who Gets Swacked, The Monster That Drank L.A.

Mercifully, the next to go was his capacity to feel despair. A soft euphoria gently muffled his anxiety, even when the hospital doctors, after those long examinations, tried to explain: "Some people's hearts grow old before their time, Mr. Montague. With others, it's the lungs or the liver. With you, it's well, it's just — how old are you? thirty-five? yes — well, what it is, you see, is that your brain, you might say, is growing older faster than the rest of you. You may as well go home," they said, "we've done all we can."

In the months that followed, his speech narrowed down to monosyllables, walking became laborious and a hazard, cigarettes dropped from his numbed fingers, memory dimmed and darkened, and he could not concentrate on the sentences in books or magazines long enough to retain the syntax. Control over the homeliest functions stopped. Long since, carnal desire had quietly deserted him. There was no pain, however. There was never any pain. Finally, he was admitted to The Home.

He had been there almost six months before Horne had garnered the courage to visit him. The place did not smell like a hospital, it smelled like something else — Horne could not identify it at first — and it was chillingly clean, the air itself was sterilized. Once inside, you were vacuum-sealed within a closed, protected, regulated world of mostly metal. A plane, that's what it smelled like, the interior of a jet liner. Its destination was Death; it was an old peoples' home. Sexless mummies crept or were wheeled silently through its corridors. A nice place, if you liked morgues. Walking up to Chet's bed had been something like walking up to an open coffin, but much worse. Pre-senile dementia had been one of the hideous terms the doctors had used, but now Chet did not resemble an old man quite so much as he resembled an infant. Like an infant, he could not sit up and he could not speak. Like an infant, he had to be fed — liquids. His eyes, like an infant's, were unfocussed, and wobbled at random in the sockets. He mimicked as an infant does, too: faintly smiled when Horne smiled, feebly nodded when Horne nodded, weakly waved when Horne, leaving, waved a last goodbye. Through the entire shattering visit, an aura of total helplessness and blind trust had emanated from Chet, and this had been the most infantile of all. "Hi, Chet, you old devil." No reaction. "It's me. Clay." Nothing. "How you keepin', tiger?" A swallowing and a spasm-flutter of the eyes. "Do you know me, Chet? Clay, Clay Horne?" The tiny nod that had only been a mirroring of Horne's own impulsive, urgent nodding as he desperately repeated, "Do you know me? Do you remember me? Chet? Chet? Do you?" Two weeks ago, that had been . . .

The coffee's umber essence filled the kitchen. Horne turned off the bubbling pot. Two weeks ago . . .

Amd now, tonight — what had he seen tonight, seen and talked with as in better days? A figment spawned by his own fervent wishes, by the wound of his anguish, by his guilt at being whole while his friend's brain calcified and shrank, his friend's mind crumbled into ash. That was one explanation, the "logical" one. Horne rejected it.

As he picked up his clammy, wrinkled clothes from the bathroom floor and climbed into them, Why *not* a ghost? he asked himself.

If there are ghosts — and damn all fools who say with narrow certainty there are none — why not a ghost of Chet? Must every molecule of flesh be cold before a ghost can be born? Who says so? What authority? What rules states this, what law?

by Ray Russell

He stepped out of the house. The night air stung him. If spirit is mind, and mind is brain, and a brain be all but snuffed out, he asked, then why may not a ghost be formed, a ghost composed of that which is already dead, those faculties forever dark, the part of Chet that mattered, not heart or blood or bowels or other stinking slimes and jellies, but the true part, the smart part, the silly part, the part that was him, the part that was happy and furious and sad, the part I knew, and knew me?

Why not? he kept demanding, in the car, driving down dead streets aglow with lunar frost, to a little all-night store he knew of. There he would buy Chet's brand of cigarettes, and his favorite gin, and smoked oysters, and Macadamia nuts, and those awful sesame crackers of which he had been inordinately fond. Ghosts eat and drink? Horne laughed. Of course not! All the same, the nuts and gin and other stuff would be there, in the house, day and night from now on, a courtesy, a sign of welcome, waiting for the return Horne hoped would happen soon, and often, and always. 🕷

✍ *Ray was the fiction editor of* Playboy *when Charles Beaumont began to slip into premature senility, and Ray said he knew something was wrong when the submissions started to lose polish, as the story says. Sad and beautiful,* n'est-ce pas?

GHOSTS IN THE MACHINE

Only Hollywood has the money to blow
on technological miracles
that only Hollywood has a use for:
A triumph! In realistic! Spectral effects! . . .
The crew has long since become inured,

but the lead actress has no clue, and
that's what counts.
Beneath the hot lights,
the camera records her hesitant steps,
dolly rolling silently beside her on its track.

The crew's thaumaturge has done his work,
the chalk lines on the sound stage do a little more
than mark the placement of imaginary walls.
A thumb's-up from the thaumaturge; the actress,
in time-honored Horror fashion, timidly pushes

open the door; she's reached her mark, and CUE:
the spook machine.
What a scream!
Oh, *what a scream!*
Give her credit, she's a pro:

when she flees,
frightened out of her mind,
with airborne undead swarming about her
howling with the fury of the damned,
she sticks to her blocking.

Harvested for period costumes
and manifestations of decay,
the ghosts mob her as she hunkers down,
still screaming. Perfect! — And CUT:
reverse the machine, suck them all away.

Watching the dailies, the director gloats:
How his rivals would kill for a take like this!
Assistants nurse the actress in her trailer;
for what she's being paid, by her next scene
she'll certainly recover.

Grateful for a competitive edge, the producer
feels Big Box Office like diamonds in her pocket,
at least this once; in a year, this new effect
will be as yesterday as typewriters,
Sylvester Stallone and CGI.

— **Mike Allen**

SWEET AS THIS

by Joel McRennary

illustrated by George H. Scithers

I was casting sugar shells when Madness came to call. In all my strange life, I had never seen anything like her.

My name is Lance. I run The Sweetshop. I don't run a candy store — allow me to reiterate — I run *The* Sweetshop. When I go to those ritzy parties to demonstrate what I do and perhaps peddle some of my wares, those who haven't already heard of me are thinking that I'm one of those retail gimps doling out chocolate bars and soda dots or variations of the fake-fruit gelatin drops. I wouldn't sully my palette with such confectionery nightmares, much less sell them to anyone else.

True, there was a time when I was forced to sell lesser products to people who didn't know any better, but that was a means to an end . . . this end. Since opening The Sweetshop back in the fall of '82, I had invented and perfected dozens of techniques in confectionery artistry, all of them costly and often very exotic. I cater mostly to the upper crust, people who want to impress other people. You know the type. But anyone who has the money and the balls to come looking for me will never walk away unsatisfied.

I should make that my mission statement.

How this woman found me I will never know. Usually, people will make appointments to view my gallery. I was sitting in a large red armchair reading a well-worn copy of *Through the Looking Glass*, waiting for my baking timer to spring, when the wooden door whispered open and a female shadow entered, followed by a cherubic little girl of perhaps seven or eight years of age. Everything about the woman glittered darkly like a starry night, and a smell like sandalwood emanated from the pair of them. The girl was bright blonde and blue-eyed, and wore a dirty smock. She seemed happy, with a lingering smile that gave the impression that she had been laughing not long ago, or was about to laugh at something.

This was despite the fact that she was leashed by a golden chain and had a clasp about her neck. Mortified, I glanced up to see the woman. She was shy of twenty — far too young to be the mother, clad in varying shades of black and blue silk. Her lengthy hair was moonlit pale, and her eyes were ashen gray. She was built quite nicely, her shape a languid curve as if her body had been balanced on the finger of a goddess.

They did not look at me, but paced idly around the glass cases, eyeing my candies — the piecemeal machinations of sugar-shell dragonflies and beetles painted with iridescent, edible lacquer; the sugar-glass marbles that imprisoned fresh berries in their centers; the Turkish chocolate drops filled with nectar of peach rose, or honeysuckle, or fresh mint leaves, or a type of delectable minced bean soaked in cinnamon oil.

My attire was as stylishly meticulous as my creations. I wore a pair of loose black Armani casuals and a black-and-gray vertically striped dress shirt, custom tailored. I was playing off the old red-and-white stripes of the stereotypical candy-jerk, but nobody ever caught onto that. My black hair was a comfortably short muss that I run my fingers through whenever I meet a pretty lady . . . like now.

"You are Lance Kinderburn," the woman said. It wasn't a question. She weighed my name on her tongue as if it were the cherry on an ice-cream sundae; to hear it shaped by that voice sent warmth thrilling down my spine. "These are very pretty," she said. "But I get the feeling that you have more to offer."

"My dear lady," I replied, standing and pocketing the book in one fluid movement, "that depends upon your level of involvement. Do you have a card?" To each of my clients I give three cards. To each of my clients I say to give the blue one to an acquaintance, the green one to a trusted friend, and the black one to an implicit confidante. This way I knew who to trust and who to razzle-dazzle. The woman had a black card in her possession, and I just had to smile.

"My name is Madeline Llwellyn; my friends call me Madness," she said, stroking the hair of her pet girl affectionately. "These same friends tell me that you are the finest candy maker and chocolatier in this city." Did I detect a hint of doubt?

"Perhaps you would like to see for yourself," I offered. Madness nodded pleasantly, and followed me into the next room, tugging the girl along. The room was undecorative to a fault. There were long glass desks, sinks, kitchen islands, small vats, a segregated laboratory, and a row of refrigerators set to different temperatures. Of course, everything was immaculately sterile.

"Please excuse the clutter, Missus Llwellyn. This is my workshop, where nearly everything gets put together," I said with a grand flourish.

"It's *Miss* Llwellyn, but please call me Madness." A lesser man would have laughed. "What made you decide to become a candy-maker, Lance?"

"Have you ever read the book *Charlie and the Chocolate Factory?*" I asked.

"No."

"Well, in the book, a little boy named Charlie inherits a chocolate and candy factory from the eccentric Willy Wonka. For as long as I can remember, I have always wanted to be that little boy. In the process I seem to have become quite an eccentric myself, selling my candies only to those who can properly appreciate the skill and effort that goes into each one."

"Or to those who can afford them?" Madness said, teasingly.

"That, too," I admitted. "Though it is not my desire to mass produce, I must say that there are not many among the *nouveau riche* that I would consider connoisseur material. But there is another reason for The Sweetshop's exclusivity . . . trust."

We reached another door. This one would only open with a password. I turned and faced the odd pair. "There are things inside this room which may not be suitable for youngsters, perhaps . . . ?"

"You needn't fear for the girl's finer sensibilities, Lance," Madness said hurriedly. "She's seen more than you would guess. Let's press on now, shall we?"

Right. Silly me. The girl seemed more on the verge of laughter than ever. I punched the password into the tiny black keypad: TEMPTING. The door hissed open to reveal a sleek chrome elevator with a sky-blue padded interior. I motioned for them to step in. "Ladies first." I lifted a secret latch behind the balance bar, and the back of the elevator swung open.

"The Xanadu Collection," I announced proudly.

The room was lighted with hidden fluorescents that gave the atmosphere a distinct ambience. Mist from the dry-ice chests crawled and licked sinuously at our feet. The room was cold, but devoid of heavy moisture, making it a bearable temperature. I explained that the cold was necessary for preserving the valuable merchandise. They didn't seem to mind at all.

With gusto, I launched them into a ten-city tour of my favorite innovations. Moving rapidly from one crystal case to the next, I showed them a clockwork merry-go-round which was made entirely of "rock" candy (it was actually a finely diluted glucose solution poured into model casts and dehydrated, reason being that I find sugar crystals and starchy syrups to be far too clumsy for my purposes). They saw the Glymmerling Set, composed of dozens of sweet jewels that shone in the light like tiny starlets (made with a specially synthesized phosphorescent compound which was safe for consumption). I introduced Madness to The Wonderland Box . . . one of my personal favorites.

The Box was shaped like a mushroom cap topped with a foil print. It depicted Alice leaning over a gigantic mushroom to speak with the hookah-smoking caterpillar. It opened from the center, the bisected lid revealing another top with an image on either side, of the Mad Hatter and the March Hare, labeled respectively "to grow" and "to shrink."

"I could really get in trouble for selling this boxed set," I explained, sliding the two sides back into the open lids. I always did enjoy a puzzle.

"The chocolates on this side are made from Austrian Godiva. The other side is coated with a special German semi-sweet, the finest to be found in Europe, and only on the black market."

"A risky confection, indeed," said Madness.

"There's more," I added. "Nestled inside are deadly amanita and psilocybin mushrooms soaked in flavored Italian syrups. The chocolate is cold sealed so that heat doesn't kill the spores. This set is made for those with a sweet-tooth for the psychedelic, so to speak."

"How very . . . interesting."

The strange duo viewed my entire selection of mind-expanding delicacies. I ran them through a gamut of aphrodisiac wonders and clever novelties. They taste-tested some of my greatest creations — from my "Nipples of Venus" to my candied roses and back to frosted finger-cakes that many attested brought them close to Nirvana. I admit that I did show them more than what I usually would for a black-card holder, but this alluring young woman and her grinning rug rat needed to become true believers. They seemed moderately impressed, but nothing close to what I was used to.

I was explaining my method for collecting nectar (genetically enhanced bees with larger honey stomachs and less enzyme production, so that they deposit more nectar into their hives than they can digest into honey) when Madness suddenly changed the subject on me.

"Do you work on commission?" she asked.

"Commission? You mean . . . special requests?" I said. How much more special could my candies get, seriously? Some people are always wanting more. "No. I have never done commissioned work . . . Why?"

"I'm hosting a gathering . . . of a sort . . . and I need a unique treat prepared for my . . . guests," she said. Her expression was dubious, almost pained, as if she were giving away a secret. She handed the other end of her leash to the girl. "You see, Lance, I've been everywhere — and please believe that I *mean* everywhere — and my efforts have only produced a few hopefuls. Perhaps you are the only one who can carry out my special need."

She sidled up close to me. Her breath smelled like wildflowers. Please God, I thought, don't let her say my name again or I'm a goner.

"Money is no object, and any other reward you would desire is negotiable," she said.

"What did you have in mind?"

"I like that . . . agreeable but not fawning. Have you ever candied insects, Lance?"

"Once or twice. They've proved a bit unrefined for my tastes."

"If I said that there was a method for candying insects — monarch butterflies in particular — while keeping them alive and fully functional, would you be interested?"

"That's a pointless question . . . it can't be done. It's been tried before, but I've never thought to waste time on it," I said. Before I had even finished this sentence, Madness had produced from the folds of her layered gown a small black box. I gave a disapproving chuckle.

She opened the lid, and immediately, a black-yellow-and-red winged butterfly fluttered out in a desperate attempt to escape. But it was tied by a tiny thread to the inside of the box. Snatching it delicately, Madness brought it to her mouth, and bit off one of the wings. Crunch. Crunch.

"Jesus —"

"It's perfectly alright," she said defensively. "You must try it." She held the butterfly out thrashing pathetically in her palm, its single wing seesawing back and forth.

"I most certainly will *not*," I replied, stepping away from her.

"You must understand what a delicious treat you could create, as sweet as this."

"I think you had better leave . . . now."

The light left her eyes. She nodded to her chattel girl, who handed her the gold leash and took the black box without a questioning glance. "Very well," she replied icily. "I thought that an artist with your vision would be enthralled with this concept. But then, I have been wrong before. Sorry for wasting your time, Mister Kinderburn."

Her black heels ticked over the floor, with the girl plodding softly along behind her. Who was this woman, to walk into *my* establishment and accuse me of lacking vision? What the hell. Worst thing I could get would be a bad taste in my mouth and the satisfaction of having tossed them out feet first.

"Wait," I said. Madness and the girl paused. "Wait. Let me try. I must be out of my mind, but I'm willing to try anything at least once." Madness smiled lazily and motioned the girl to present me with the butterfly. It flip-flopped into my hand, and without stopping to think about it — I tossed it into my mouth and bit down.

And the width and breadth of my perceptual sphere locked in a moment of pure, breathless ecstasy. Fireworks of pleasure were going off in my brain as my blind and befuddled tongue fitfully explored this new morsel. This taste wasn't just high on the spectrum, it *was* the spectrum. It was the rainbow and the shadow and the smooth taste of darkness and sunshine. It was the equivalent of spasmodic sex with a virgin Calypso on the back of a racing Harley tearing up the stars in a violent explosion of beauty and violence and magic. All five senses were massaged by the soft traces of perfection.

The taste . . . I just couldn't put my finger on it. Whatever it was, it shamed sugar, chocolate, berries, spices, and nectar. I felt a passing twinge of regret when I realized that I would never be able to reach any sort of climax without comparing it with this.

I felt myself drifting. I actually started to *see* things, to hallucinate. I saw willowy, dancing girls with wings, naked and laughing. I saw boys, clever and shifty-eyed and utterly dangerous. I saw Madness, blowing her sweet breath into my face and bringing me back into focus with what I used to call the real world.

My brain wanted to reboot, to go back to the square one of Lance Kinderburn: Professional Candy-man and Artiste Extraordinaire. But I had tasted ambrosia of the gods, and I knew that there was no turning back. I sunk to my knees, into the dry-ice mist, and started crying like a newborn baby.

The deal went as follows: I was to candy eighteen live butterflies in two weeks, using six preservatives and the special ingredient provided in a purple glass vial. There was plenty of room for artistic license, and if I did it to her specifications, Madness would let me keep what was left of the special ingredient, which she called ichor.

I threw myself into this new project with uninhibited fervor, casting aside all others. To work on the insects, I prepared a mixture of 0.25 cc's of ether to one part spring water, sprayed one of the butterflies with an atomizer, and waited for temporary paralysis to set in. The first order of business was the easiest — candying the wings. A butterfly's wings are coated with tiny scales that contain pigment. These scales can be quite easily brushed off, so it was a very tentative operation. A fine, sweet powder (corn starch, glucose, sugar, and ichor mixed and brought to a boil, dried, and mortared) is placed in a dram spoon and lightly blown with a straw at an angle where it fixes under their scales.

Now, before you get the idea that I went on a country outing to chase around a bunch of stupid butterflies, banish the thought. Madness provided them, specially fed as caterpillars on milkweed that had been watered with ichor. It took one whole day to candy a single butterfly, and the worst part of it was that I had no way of knowing if

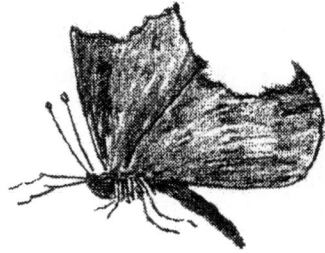

I had done it right.

I stepped into my study to reflect on the events of the day, trying to put all my thoughts in order, but all I could do was fantasize about tasting the ichor. I lit a cigarette and started pacing. I usually kept them for guests, never being a smoker myself.

The next ten days skipped by like flat stones on the still surface of time. With each delicate little insect I powdered and glazed and injected, I got a little better and the job went faster. Unfortunately, that gave me room in my head to think about the mechanics of this whole bizarre charade.

Messages were stockpiling on the answering machine. The workshop was in total disarray. Pans stagnated in the sink, Chinese take-out boxes and scribbled notes littered the drafting table, and the oven stank with the sugar shells I had burnt on the day Madness had visited me. I was powdering the wings of the eighth butterfly, my fingers moving with a surgeon's practiced dexterity. A bit of powder touched my index finger, and I absently sucked it clean. I shut my eyes tight and savored every grain and molecule, the flavor not as strong as before, but just as fulfilling. The things I could make with just a single drop of this stuff, I thought. But the leftovers in that bottle would only last so long, and who would be privileged enough to enjoy it? Money and fame wavered like mirage-forms before me, but those dreams left a bad taste in my mouth, and I'd had my fill of both. The desk telephone startled me by ringing. I snatched it up feverishly. "Hello?"

"Do you have any clue what you've involved yourself in?" The voice was young, and unnaturally bright considering the gravity of the statement. "If you are wise, you'll listen to me. If you run, they will find you. If you break your promise, you'll die."

"Very well," I replied skeptically. "I'm listening."

One step took me outside, into the sunlight. Despite the fact that my skin was pale and one could almost make out the veins beneath, and my eyes looked like two dark sores — I felt like a trillion bucks. The previous night was spent adding the final artistic touches to my masterpiece. Colors were dueling in the sky, deep blue battling pure white and finally embracing across the sunlit fields of oblivion. I could smell the fishery across the street, the bubble-gum being chewed in the mouth of a teenage girl speeding by on roller-skates, the sun baking the blacktop.

For this very special outing, I was wearing a black London Fog overcoat with hooks instead of buttons. On my head was a hands-free cell-phone, and gripped in my right hand I held a small birdcage filled with eighteen candied butterflies. On my chest I felt the potent weight of a .44 magnum thump with every stride. My hands-free rang. I answered it.

"Madness here," her voice resounded in my skull like poetry. "Are you ready to begin?" For this client I agreed to deliver her candies personally. For this client I agreed to follow her instructions to bring them to where she was hosting her "gathering."

"You know," I said, "if I'm going to be walking down Seventh Avenue talking to myself and carrying a birdcage, must I keep calling you Madness?"

"Clever . . . turn right into the alley beside the bakery," she replied.

"I was wondering. Where does the ichor come from, how do you get it?"

"Rare plants, off the coast of Borneo . . . go up the steps at the end and into the door."

"Interesting. I've read up on some things about rabbinic mythology and 'ichor' — if you will — is another name for the blood of the angels. Are you interested in the occult, Miss Llwellyn?"

"I would think that to be obvious, Lance." Her voice was smiling gently. "Turn right down the hall and into another alley, then left." The hall was soggy plaster falling into dusty crumbs. There was a doorway at the end of the hall. I stepped through it.

"There is nothing obvious about you, Miss Llwellyn, trust me. I always check out my clients before giving them an appointment, or after — in your case." The alley was dark and moist and very unpleasant smelling. Couldn't there have been another way to get there? "I found it odd that none of my twenty-five hundred clients have ever registered a Madeline Llwellyn."

"Perhaps he forgot . . . go down the steps. It's an old subway station."

Indeed it was an old subway of the most abandoned nature. There was garbage and slag everywhere, and the air smelled like dust getting cooped up and claustrophobic. Gang symbols decked the shadowy walls. That darkness, hell — anything could be in there. I patted my gun-thick chest for reassurance. "What do I do now, Miss Llwellyn?"

Silence was my answer. The butterflies were going crazy in their cage, and I was not going to take the blame if one of them damaged itself. It was when I heard the dial tone beeping like an alarm in my ear that I knew I was in trouble. The shadows were starting to scurry and move all around me. "Who's there?" I cried. I set down the cage and pulled out my .44. "Back away," I said. "I'm not kidding."

"If you would like to make a call, please hang up and dial again. This is a recording."

One of the shadows pounced in my direction, and I fired twice. **Blam. Blam.** The gunshots exploded in the near pitch darkness. My ears rang and my whole body turned into a hot iron. The shadow was flung back into obscurity. I heard a loud thud, and a dull pain washed over my head as my own consciousness fell into obscurity.

When I awoke, it was to the mellow flush of candlelight blooming all around me. I was trussed up on the dirty concrete like a Christmas parcel. The cage of butterflies was a few feet away, surrounded by figures I first thought to be products of my damaged brain.

"I see you have awakened, Lance . . . good. We thought we had killed you." I didn't need to look up, but I did anyway. Madness stood there in all her seductive glory, seeming more to pity me than triumphant. Beside her stood a handsome man who looked straight out of *A Midsummer Night's Dream.* He wore a pair of healthy ram's horns and his legs were that of the same. Scattered about were similar creatures, two beautiful girls in faded shifts and tunics with flowing, bright hair and delicate wings, three young men with wise grins that surpassed their years. They were the ones from my vision. There was a subtle power that radiated from their presence, something glamorous yet disturbingly ancient.

"Surprised, Lance? Don't look so betrayed. . . . You didn't do all that work for nothing," said Madness. "We need the butterflies for the ritual . . . almost as much as we need you. You see, we can't let you use the ichor for your sweets. It's much too precious for that. It is literally the blood of the angels, tapped by our patron goddess, Lilith, at the dawning of humanity." I did not like the sound of that.

The creatures slowly gathered into a circle. The goat-man began singing passages out of a great, dusty tome. His voice was low and sonorous. The others began leaping about in synchronicity, weaving their hands around the center of their circle. The ground began to shimmer, and the sharp tang of ozone flooded my senses. Then, the goat-man stopped, and began speaking in English. "Every seven years since the dawning of our breed from the womb of Lilith, a tithe has been set unfairly upon us by Him whose name must not be spoken. We have come into this place of foul human creation to pay this debt, that the King of the Damned may be appeased." Following this statement, each of them took a butterfly from the cage and ate it. The munching sound was disgusting.

Why couldn't anything in my life be normal? Would they force me to partake in their ritual, pollute my spirit with intoxicating magic that would bind me to them forever? Would I become a mindless, grinning slave like the little blond girl?

One of the elf creatures came towards me and pulled a wicked dagger from his belt. Madness stooped down and kissed me on the cheek, but I was numb to it. "Try to make it quick, Tormel."

The elf creature leaned in close, his breath smelled like campfire. "You shot my brother, man-thing, now your head must come off . . . slowly."

"Wait," I cried. "There's no ichor left . . . I drank it all. Look in my eyes and you'll know it's true." Behind Tormel, Madness stumbled to her knees and the goat-man braced himself against the wall.

"I have no doubt it is . . . I'm still going to kill you."

"But don't you want to know my secret ingredient, Peter Pan?" Tormel placed the edge of his knife on my throat, but I just smiled at him. "It's concentrated hemlock . . . enough to kill a horse and certainly enough to kill whatever you are."

As if he thought I was bluffing, he turned to see his companions twitching in the rubble. He should have killed me when he had the chance. Turning drunkenly, gripping his dagger with grim determination, he brought the knife up. Falling backwards, Tormel was dead before he hit the ground.

I heaved a sigh of relief. I never thought that I would have lived this long. *First order of business now is to find some way to get out of these ropes*, I thought. Suddenly, I realized that there was one figure left standing. From out of the shadow of an overturned subway car stepped the little blonde girl, still chained at the neck.

She walked calmly to the body of her mistress and touched her face. I watched in suspended anxiety as she kissed Madness's cheek, and rose with Tormel's dagger in hand. Crouching close, she swiped the blade across my chest. A tiny trickle of blood inched down my belly.

"You have to take care of me now," she said. I looked down and felt the ropes slacken and fall away. "You promised you would . . . on the phone," she added, frowning.

"Sweetie," I replied, lifting myself up and staggering slightly, "I'll do much more than that." Having better night vision than I, she led the way out. "I always thought that The Sweetshop needed a more youthful touch, something to break the tedium and introduce some unpredictability. If you prove to be a quick study, you may even be better than me someday."

"Really, you'll give me your candy store?" she said with sprightly excitement.

"Sweetshop, dear . . . *The* Sweetshop," I replied. "If you remember *anything* I tell you at all, please try to remember *that.*"

🕷

✍ *Joel McRennary is a Kentucky native, but he reserves the right to be a native of any other place at any given time. He currently resides in Louisville with his wife, dog, and two ancient cats. He is an undergraduate working towards a degree in English studies. He has written verse for* Choice Digest *and fiction for* Kentucky's Best Writing and Art.

He plans to use his found-object, post-modern art to support his true passion: writing fantasy and horror.

KILLING THE PAIN

by Marc Bilgrey

illustrated by Mike Dubisch

We'd been married for ten years and were living in Los Angeles, when she left me. I woke up one day and she was gone. A short note explained that the other guy was an actor, just like me, only more successful. Like a fool, I waited a month for her to come back. When she didn't, I went home to New York.

She was my whole life. I loved her more than I'd ever loved anyone. I suppose I should have seen it all coming, but I hadn't. Sure, there'd been tension, I'd only been working sporadically; bit parts in sit-coms, under fives in movies, a few commercials. It had always been a struggle and she hated waitressing. In the last year jobs were even harder to find. My agent dropped me. My wife became emotionally distant, and started spending a lot of time out of the house.

So, there I was, in Manhattan, for the first time in a decade. At forty, I felt alone, lost, like an alien from another planet. I thought the familiarity of the city I'd grown up in would offer me some spiritual solace, but that proved elusive. It wasn't the same place I'd left. Many of the stores and restaurants I'd remembered were gone and most of the people I knew, all New York transplants, were back in L.A.

Through a newspaper ad I found a small apartment on the upper west side that I shared with a graduate student from Columbia. He was seldom home, and when he was, he spent his time studying.

I felt as if I were in a surreal dream. Everything reminded me of my wife. Daisies outside the neighborhood grocery store (they were her favorite flower), a pair of shoes in a shop window. I could no longer listen to music without crying.

The days became endless. I went to auditions, no longer caring if I got the roles. The nights were worse. Either I couldn't sleep at all, or I awoke every two or three hours. Often, I'd take long walks through the deserted streets.

It occurred to me that I had to kill the pain or I couldn't go on. I considered drinking, but the idea appealed only in theory. The thought of actually getting drunk on an ongoing basis seemed pointless. Especially since there would always come the inevitable time when the alcohol would wear off and reality would return. Drugs, both legal and illegal, had the same inherent problem. Besides, I reasoned, I wanted real escape, not a temporary diversion.

I thought about sex, except for the first time in my life, I had no interest in it. That, and the only woman I could think about was my wife.

I mulled over seeing a shrink, but couldn't afford one, which was just as well, as I had little faith in the talking cure, anyway.

I came up with the bright idea that maybe religion could help. After all, I thought, it had brought great comfort to millions of people throughout the ages. I went to a few churches during off-hours, hoping for some kind of divine salvation, but left each one disappointed and with a deep feeling of emptiness. I envied the people I saw there who looked like true believers. They prayed to a fair and just God, apparently never doubting that he would hear their pleas, and bestow his infinite blessings upon them.

I thought about suicide. Since my wife had left, it had crossed my mind periodically. Now the thought lingered. I contemplated jumping out of a window, sticking a knife into my stomach or throwing myself into the path of an oncoming train. Unfortunately, I lacked the guts to carry out any of my self-destructive fantasies.

One afternoon, in late October, three months after arriving in the city, I found myself wandering aimlessly through the Village. I passed dozens of greeting-card stores, sex shops, retro boutiques and dimly lit capuccino bars. On a side street, I stopped in front of a metaphysical bookstore. In the window were crystals, multi-colored candles, ancient-looking hourglasses, and dusty leather bound volumes. A sign near a skull read: **PROBLEMS SOLVED, QUESTIONS ANSWERED**.

When I walked inside the store, a little bell on the door jingled. There didn't seem to be anyone around, as I went down the cramped aisles of bookshelves. I was examining a thin book that was written in a language I didn't recognize, when a voice behind me said, "May I help you?"

I turned to see a man with a closely cropped white beard, who looked like he was in his seventies. He was dressed in a black shirt and pants. Around his neck was a purple pendant.

"I'm just looking," I said.

"Is your problem love or money?" he asked.

"Love," I replied, feeling more than a bit awkward. He continued asking me questions, and before I knew it, I began telling him all about me and my wife. It felt good to be confiding in someone, especially a stranger.

When I was done he said, "Perhaps I can be of some help."

"Do you have a book of spells that'll bring my wife back?" I said, only half seriously.

"You've been seeing too many bad movies," he said, smiling. "However, you are clearly seeking an end to your suffering."

"Yes, I am." Though I hadn't said it in so many words.

"You come at a most opportune time. Tomorrow is the eve of Sauin."

"Sauin?"

"Halloween. It's the one day of the year when the connecting material between this world and the next thins. In fact, there are places where it actually tears."

I realized that had I been having this conversation a year earlier, I would probably have left at that moment. But everything had changed, and I was not willing to dismiss anything without a thorough hearing.

"The connecting material . . . ?" I said.

"I'm sure you think I sound like a lunatic, but at the same time you are intrigued or you wouldn't be in my shop." The old man touched his pendant and then continued. "Yes, tomorrow night there will be a rip in the universe."

"Why are you telling me this?" I asked.

"Because it happens that we are one person short."

"I still don't see —"

"Each year someone passes through from our side to the other world. It is an offering to the gods."

"Like a sacrifice?"

"We prefer to think of it as a gesture of good will."

"Do you kill someone?" I asked, glancing in the direction of the door.

"Certainly not," he said, squinting. "The volunteer offers himself freely and of his own will."

"And how —"

"He steps through the opening, like a birth in reverse. And then the crevice seals and he is no longer of this world."

"Is it painful?"

"Not at all. It is like shedding one set of clothes for another."

I wasn't sure if I believed a word he'd said; but the idea of someone else killing me was something I hadn't thought of before.

"Is this other world Hell?" I asked.

"The old man laughed. "Hardly. It's where the spirits dwell." He took a notebook and pen out of his pocket and wrote something down. Then he tore the page out and handed it to me. He'd written an address on Long Island.

"Get there before midnight tomorrow night," he said, turning and walking into another aisle of books.

I took a few steps and said, "But what if I don't —!" I looked around, but didn't see the old man. I checked the rest of the store, but saw no sign of him. Deciding that he must have gone into a back room, I shrugged and left the shop.

On the bus ride uptown, I clutched the paper he'd given me and stared at the address. It was in Montauk, all the way at the tip of Long Island.

What was I getting myself mixed up in? I wondered. Then again, if it turned out that his wild story was true, my torment would be over. If not, maybe he and his cult, which is certainly what it sounded like, would do me in, in the old fashioned way. In any case, the whole thing sounded very dangerous. Essentially, everything I'd been looking for.

That night, for the first time in months, I slept without interruption and awoke refreshed and with a profound sense of peace that I couldn't remember ever having experienced.

At dinner, I thought, this is the last meal I will ever eat. Afterwards, I wrote out a will, leaving my few possessions, mostly books, to friends. An hour later, I left my apartment, went to Pennsylvania Station, and bought a ticket to Montauk. While waiting for the train to be called, I saw a few small children in masks and colorful costumes. They held shopping bags and orange plastic jack-o'-lanterns.

When the train was announced, I got on slowly, having to steady my shaking hands, and found a seat. After the tunnel, the lights of Manhattan quickly faded, as the train sped into the darkness. I looked out the window at the passing houses and cars. Hours went by. When the train finally rolled into Montauk, the station was deserted.

I found a lone taxi, awakened the driver, got into the back seat, and read him the directions. He took off through the quiet streets, onto a narrow road. We drove by many white houses, which looked like summer homes. None of them had any lights on.

Fifteen minutes later, I paid the driver and was left standing on a shadowy cliffside road. In the moonlight I saw the ocean far below. The air smelled of salt water, and the only sound was the faint lapping of the waves on the beach a few hundred feet beneath me.

On the cliff were some oversized rocks and what looked like poles that had been stuck into the ground. I was trying to come up with a reason for them being there when I saw something move in the darkness.

At first, I thought it was an animal, but then, as it got closer, I saw that it was human. He was dressed in a black robe and hood, the sort that Trappist monks wear. His face was obscured in shadow. I called out, "Am I in the right place?" but he didn't answer. And then I was surrounded by more robed figures, thirteen in all. No one said a word as they formed a circle around me. Suddenly, there was a loud 'thump,' and flames shot

out of the tops of the poles in the ground.

For some seconds the robed figures stood frozen in place, then they began walking counterclockwise around me. This went on for a while till they stopped and began chanting, in what I initially thought might be Latin, but realized must've been something else. Then I heard a drum start pounding out an almost hypnotic rhythm, though I saw no drummer. To the drumming was added what sounded like small bells and some kind of flute-like instrument. I saw no source for these, either.

The chanting grew louder, as the air filled with a putrid burning smell, perhaps of a decayed animal, I don't know. One of the robed figures produced a long stick with what appeared to be a crystal at the end of it. Still staying within the circle, he leaped onto one of the rocks and held the stick toward the sky. The crystal glowed with an unearthly light.

Suddenly, I felt a cold wind cut through the air and a vortex of dried leaves began swirling around the circle. And then, all at once, everything stopped. The chanting, the music, the wind, and the flames extinguished themselves. Everyone stood silently in the moonlight. Was it over? I wondered. Would they now stab me with daggers and throw me off the cliff? Or maybe it had all simply been a lot of talk, and nothing would happen.

My thoughts were interrupted by a flash of light that lit up the night sky. I had heard of no storm warnings, I thought, as a black cloud moved swiftly across the moon. Then, to my amazement, I saw the cloud expand like a spreading inkblot.

In seconds, the moon and sky were totally enveloped in a dark, billowy fog. Then, it parted, revealing a bright red, luminous streak that looked like a burning rainbow. This 'opened' and inside were white glowing wisps of smoke.

I stood shivering as the smoke curled in my direction. Embedded inside it were hideous, distorted, maniacal faces. Green and yellow eyes glared at me, while guttural laughter echoed in the ether. The crimson streak grew nearer, and the smoke orbited around the cliff like a roulette wheel that had just been spun by an unseen croupier.

My heart jumped, as I was grabbed by two of the robed figures. This was it, I thought, while I stared into the red abyss. In a few seconds I would cease to exist.

And then I heard someone sneeze. I turned, and in the blood red light, saw the illuminated face of one of the robed figures. She was a beautiful woman. There was a gentleness to her features, a soft expression that belied her surroundings. In that instant, I thought about warm summer days in Central Park, old friends, and being with a woman who loved me and would never betray me. I realized that I didn't fear death. What I feared was life.

I turned back to the red opening that loomed in front of me. The two robed figures held me and pushed me forward. I hit one of them in the stomach and punched the other in the throat. Their grips were broken and I pulled away. I lunged straight into the others and punched and kicked like a berserker, then jumped out of the circle and ran to the road.

Behind me, I heard muffled cries and footsteps coming in my direction. I picked up my pace and sprinted ahead. The moon appeared, and in the faint light I soared past sharp brambles and pitch black houses. Within ten minutes, I managed to escape my would-be captors. Sometime later, half running, half walking, I reached a gas station and phoned for a cab. The ride back to Manhattan was uneventful.

In the weeks that followed I tried to make some sense of what had happened that night. One thing I was now sure of, the universe is a lot more mysterious, wondrous and frightening than I had ever imagined.

I also discovered something about myself. When faced with certain death, I chose life. And having done so, I decided that I had to somehow conquer my despair and ultimately move on. I came to the conclusion that I was in mourning, not for a person, but for a marriage. Mourning is not something that you can go through immediately; it's a process, it takes time and patience and understanding.

I joined a separated-and-divorced support-group, and met other people who were going through similar pain. I also signed up for an acting class, which I thought of as a celebration of life. That's not to say that everything suddenly became wonderful, it didn't. I still struggled every day with my depression, but I started having some good days, too.

One afternoon in December, I was standing on the downtown side of the Seventy-Second Street subway platform, waiting for a train, when I happened to look across the tracks at the uptown side. There, on the platform, I saw a woman staring at me. She looked familiar, but I couldn't place her. Then a chill went up my back as I recognized her. She was the woman in the robe and hood I'd seen that night. She smiled at me. A cold, cruel smile. She began moving in my direction. I went up the station stairs two at a time, ran out the exit door, into the street and got onto the first bus I could find.

✠

✍ *Marc Bilgrey's short stories have appeared in many anthologies, including* The Ultimate Halloween, Crafty Cat Crimes, The Mutant Files, *and* Merlin. *He has also written for television and comedians.*

ZOMBIE LUCK

Car engines never start
when the zombies are chasing you,
and no house key will fit in the lock

as those moaning corpses
lurch toward your front door,
and all the random turns taken as you flee

will lead you, guaranteed,
down a dead end alley.
With back against the wall,

you can only stare, sweating,
as groans with graveyard timbre
grow louder, closer,

and it just won't occur to you,
as those decayed hands grope for your throat,
that you're faster, smarter,

probably stronger, that a tug at a putrid arm
might rip it from a shoulder like tissue paper,
or a sharp kick to a desiccated knee

could snap the bone like balsa wood.
That's undead juju, you might say,
a gift from the darkest of loa

to their dumbest of slaves.
For how else could a creature so stupid and slow
so consistently capture its prey?

— **Mike Allen**

THE PRIDE IS BACK

by Jean Paiva

illustrated by David Grilla

Maybe because I never managed to get far enough away either as the crow flies or as the heart beats, it was so easy for me to return. The main reason I'd left Ridgeton in the first place was the stories. Not the only reason, by any stretch, but the handed-down and watered-down tales of hobgoblin types stealing babes from their cribs and wandering Indian ghosts sacrificing lost hikers to the sun told more about the backwater mentality than they did of local legends. The irony is that stories were also why I came back.

My own tall tales were slow to sell, probably, though it pains me to admit it, for much the same reason. In the fifteen years I'd been gone, some new material had been added to the Ridgeton general store repertoire; werewolves were big after I left and a few years ago it was alien life forms. The funny thing is that no one was even close.

This morning a blanket of insect sounds covered the woods with subdued buzzing from everywhere and nowhere, surrounding the small campsite I'd staked and claimed for my own.

But even the promised dawn on this, the fifth day of record breaking heat, hinted at no relief. It was still oven hot and sticky humid.

Half the town was camped out, as they were last night and the night before, probably lying awake like me watching the clouds race fast and low in front of the hazy moon. There could have been a dome shield between the sky and the earth; no hint of any breeze reached us. Only the silence.

Babs would never have come into the woods, but she was gone. The first pang of loss, of hurt, of pain, when I realized she'd left without so much as a note or call or message was soon replaced with an even greater sense of relief. The taste of freedom quickly grew sweet; ten long years and her seventy added pounds took enough time and space into consideration to account for my speedy recovery. If she were still here she'd have been back in town with the old and ailing and superstitious . . . all those who wouldn't come into the forest because of the fantasies idle wives wove over backyard fences.

Counting campsites, I realized that at least three people I knew of, not counting Babs, had recently disappeared without a trace. I envied them.

Thornton's youngest daughter, a nineteen-year-old with the build of a linebacker, couldn't find her niche here in Ridgeton, Kentucky, population 2870, and left a note saying she'd write when she got where she was going, as soon as she figured out where. It was two months now and there'd been no word. Last month we figured Mrs. Clifton eloped with Ned Barnes, both of them widowed less than a year. Guess they thought they'd better get out of town while the gossips had their day and would come back when it settled down. It's a sure bet they didn't climb down the traditional eloper's ladder — between them they weighed more than a quarter ton. No one had heard from them either but what can you expect from honeymooners?

I heard others were taking off, too, but didn't know their names or gossipy particulars. Just that they'd left, often without a word good-bye. Who could blame them? I wouldn't be here if I didn't have to live in the house my father left me. The bus terminal must be some busy place on Wednesdays. That's still express day, just like it was fifteen years ago when I stood, ticket in hand, high school diploma packed in my single suitcase, waiting for the overnight bus to Dayton, Ohio, so I could connect for Columbus and points unchartered. Columbus was as far as I ever got.

The smell of coffee drifted west and whetted my taste buds; it was time to decide what to do with the day. Head to a neighboring campsite and cadge a cup of coffee and then, having already made people contact, drift into town? Or move up the mountain? The lumber and paint business my dad founded still ran out of my house and it would probably keep going no matter who ran it, competition being what it wasn't; I was living proof of that. Besides, I deserved a break. It had been years since I just took off and today, if ever, was the day to go.

Half a day and a couple of miles into the woods and instead of relaxing I was thinking of the untended store and the blank piece of paper in my typewriter and feeling guilty, almost but not quite ready to turn around. Didn't much matter, I reminded myself; lunch was in the bag but I had to go back for supper, anyhow.

Finding a comfortable spot to unpack my hard-boiled eggs and peanut-butter sandwich was easy. As soon as I thought of food I sat under the nearest tree, leaned against the rugged bark and stretched out. Staying relaxed wasn't so easy.

A sudden screech like a chainsaw thrown into gear and revved up to high cut harshly through the dense growth of trees. It happened so quickly the sound surrounded me, no direction discernible, and lasted for maybe a minute. Then it repeated itself twice and from much closer echoed back, the final note hanging in the suddenly still air. Someone, I was sure, was cutting firewood with a faulty power tool — even though that was a cool weather task. But the sounds didn't pick up again. Maybe they were just testing their saw but then I realized I couldn't think of anyone living out this far. Besides, sounds didn't travel very far in dense woods. Animals? Nothing that large has been seen in these woods for the last twenty years. The spreading homesteads and towns pushed the cougars and bears into the upstate mountains and narrowed the forest here to no more than twenty miles deep at the widest point.

Still, my nerves were jumping and wouldn't relax until I looked around. Wrapping the sandwich, I got up to explore the area. Pushing my way through the bushes I expected anything but what I saw. The lumber business I sort of ran gave me the bare bones of an idea what it took to build a house; the four by fours and two by fours and siding and framing and shingling, not to mention the massive amounts of miscellaneous hardware it took to construct a frame. How someone got that much lumber this far into the woods, with no roads, was completely beyond me . . .

The house was more modern than mine. A long low wood-frame building with a stone base, I counted seven windows on the side nearest —

two of them full length double doors — and five more windows on the front. An elaborate wooden door bracketed by two stained glass panels I didn't include in my window count and a heavy stone chimney jutting up from the far side completed the picture. There was only about ten feet between the house and the woods on all sides, with manicured bushes trailing into and becoming part of the wild growth of the forest.

What the hell, I thought — there wasn't much else I could think — and walked to the front door.

Up close, the polished mahogany front door doubled as a relief sculpture of a lion's head. The snarling muzzle, in the midst of a roar, was at least three feet high, and a flowing mane curved and curled into surrounding vines. The lion's bared teeth were inlaid, bone or ivory or, looking closer, maybe even real teeth. I took a step back, just in case. The brass knocker was on the side and it, too, was of a lion's head. No teeth were bared on the knocker, so I used it.

I heard the creak of floorboards as the door swung slowly open. No "Who's there?" piped from the other side, but this wasn't extra-cautious Columbus, it wasn't even downtown Ridgeton.

She stood there in cut offs, shorts clipped from well worn jeans, starting below the navel and with no more than four inches of denim from waistband to frayed edge. A minimum coverage for flawless flesh. I'm not sure why my stare started there because, as my eyes lifted to the halter-type top that was jury-rigged from some sort of sheer scarf and then to the heart-shaped face with tilted gold-flecked eyes surrounded by a mass of tawny hair, I knew I wanted to keep looking at the whole as well as the parts for a long time.

The smile that touched the corners of her full lips was encouraging, but I couldn't think of anything to say. Tongue-tied is the phrase. Instead, I smiled back, which was the right thing to do, and put out my hand, which was the wrong thing to do. She startled, sounding a soft hiss of air and jumped back from the door while moving her hands palms out, fingers curled, as if to push me away, or claw me. I looked at her narrowed eyes and my outstretched hand, now sinking timidly to my side, and finally found something to say.

"I'm sorry, I didn't mean to frighten you," I apologized. It must have been the right thing to say. She blinked, twice, the smile slowly returning to that wonderful mouth, and her hands lowered to her side.

"No, I'm sorry," she replied in a silky near-whisper tinged with the slightest accent. "We so rarely get visitors, I don't know what I was thinking."

The "we" stood out like a blinking stoplight on a deserted highway; it echoed and bounced off rapidly shattering fantasies, my dream embrace of her tender flesh was the first vision to crack under its harsh sound. *We.*

"I should have guessed, had I taken half a minute to think about it," I answered while the last vision I'd invented in the 30 seconds I wasn't thinking crumbled into dust. "You're sort of out-of-the way here," I lamely concluded.

"You're the first stranger to find us in five years," she said, "and only about the seventh visitor this year." The faint accent was unknown to me, but I haven't heard many foreigners speak. She could even have been American and have lived abroad for a time. She looked into my face, finding, I guess, the arrangement that I'd been told was ruggedly handsome and what I thought more of a nuisance to shave, acceptable.

"Yes, the seventh," she said, not moving from the doorway.

"I'm from Ridgeton, I run the lumber business there," I started to say as I watched her smile grow. It took my breath away and any other words I had evaporated.

After waiting a decent interval for me to continue, which I didn't, she shook her head, further tousling her already electric hair. "Well, we don't need any lumber," she said in the same silky voice, ending her words in almost a purr. "We've got plenty around us."

My wits returned, sort of, and I smiled back. "This isn't a sales call. I mean, I didn't come here to sell you anything. I didn't even know you, anyone, was here. Just walking the woods to stay cool," I admitted, and then fully realized what I'd really said. "I should have heard about you. No one knows there's a house here. How did you get this built?"

"Oh, they brought the lumber up in tractors from the highway near Glenndale as far as the first ridge, then on pulleys after that. My husband and I wanted privacy," she added, looking directly at me with, I thought, a bit less of a smile.

"Of course. I'm sorry to have bothered you, I mean I just saw the house and my curiosity got the best of me."

"Well," she said, reaching a graceful hand with its long slender nails to me, "you're here now and curiosity has its own rewards. You may as well come in and recover from your hike. I know how far it is. Would you like some coffee, or a cool

drink, before you start back?"

Her grip was surprisingly strong and her nails, as one nicked my bare forearm, amazingly sharp. After the privacy bit I was surprised to be invited in but wasn't about to pass on the offer.

"I'd love a cool drink," I said and followed her as she moved stealthily on bare feet toward the kitchen area. The room must have been half the house, spacious and open and reaching as far back as the glass doors and giant fireplace. Couches, chairs, small tables and large cushions were scattered around, the furniture on the polished wood floor and cushions on the overlapping carpets and animal skin rugs. Trinkets covered the tables and bowls filled with small souvenirs sat on the long cabinet set against the far wall. Above the cabinet, mounted animal heads lined the wall separating this room from the back of the house. A musky odor, too harsh to be her perfume, lay over the room.

"My name is Martin Kyle," I said, hoping the introduction would prompt conversation. "I didn't expect to find anything like this house, or you, today. This is a great room," I said as I walked to the trophy wall. It took a minute before it registered. These weren't stuffed deer or moose or your other standard trophies. These were from the big jungles of Africa. Dead center, no pun intended, was the largest lion's head I'd ever seen. But then I couldn't think of another stuffed lion's head I'd ever seen. In fact, outside the Columbus zoo I hadn't seen any live ones either. The giant maned head was frozen in an roar and bracketed on either side by smaller, smooth-furred heads which in turn were followed by even smaller heads of unfamiliar but vicious looking creatures.

"This is some terrific lion," I said, somewhat lamely. "What are the rest of these heads?"

"Those are three lions, a male and two of his mates. The others are just some wildebeests," she answered, finishing setting up the coffee pot to perk and crossing the room to me. "We got them in Kenya."

I must have looked at her strangely, wondering how people who had traveled as far as Africa would not only end up here, near Ridgeton, but here in the middle of nowhere. She laughed, which told me I was on good footing.

"I'm Aurora Milner. I trapped these lions as cubs and trained them." She paused, looking at the heads with affection. "For the circus, of course. These were the first three I raised, my children really, and I wanted to remember them.

They performed before crowned heads." She turned to face me, never taking her eyes off mine, and gracefully gestured with her right arm. Muscles I hadn't noticed before tensed and looked firm enough to crack a whip or subdue most men at arm wrestling, though no matter how many lions she could whip into place her real strength was in her eyes. They were as amber as ripened grain rippling like a field of wheat in a soft summer breeze.

"Where's your husband now?" I asked, not only because it was the logical question but because I felt my soul being pulled into her and was afraid my body would soon follow.

"Tracking," she said, looking directly back into my eyes.

"Here?" I was barely able to ask.

"In the woods," she answered, moving, to my immediate and everlasting gratitude, closer to me. Her scent was of the forest, pine and musk, deep and cloying, intoxicating.

"Nearby?"

"Within a few miles."

"Oh," I concluded, my mind not working any quicker than my tongue.

Within a few miles meant anywhere from five minutes to five hours, and the thought of facing her husband, a lion trainer, was more effective than a cold shower. I backed away, finding myself up against the long cabinet under the mounted heads. Turning my back to her was the most difficult thing I can remember ever doing but I did. Needing a diversion, I started playing with the trinkets in the large bowl: carved figures of ivory and ebony, perfectly formed sea shells and chunks of what I knew must be coral reef, smooth polished bangles carved with intricate designs or set in silver. Picking up a shell, I was about to ask where it came from when a glint of gold caught my eye; there was a piece of something sticking out between a carved disk and some coral.

What I could see looked like half a heart and my thoughts jumped to Babs and the locket she always wore — the locket I had given her for our engagement. Reaching to push the coral away, I felt rather than saw Aurora move closer to me and my attention shifted to her presence, and wondered what to do about it.

I did the only sensible thing and turned to face her with open arms.

Hours later, when my stomach let loose a rumble, I remembered my lunch had gone uneaten.

Aurora's head, resting on my chest, her tawny hair spread from my shoulders to my navel, shot up — her eyes again narrowed, her hand a talon grip on the part of me she had been gently caressing. As tears of pain came to my eyes, all thoughts of food forgotten, she relaxed and once again blessed me with her smile.

"You haven't eaten." Her lilting accent was stronger now, or perhaps I was listening closer. "I'll make us lunch."

It was closer to dinner, but anything she wanted to call it as long as it was food was fine. Thinking about dinner also made me remember the trek down the mountain, one best accomplished in daylight. Thoroughly comfortable, propped up on soft pillows with a gentle cool breeze waving lace curtains, satiated for the first time in months, I thought about the effort it would take to get up. It was now late afternoon and, allowing for the meal, I would have just enough time to cover the few miles to Ridgeton by dusk. I could probably find my way in the dark by just heading down, but then again maybe not. Besides, I remembered, and was out of bed in about two seconds flat, her husband should be home any time.

"Food sounds great," I said to cover my nervousness. "What's cooking?" Slipping into my shirt, I felt the fabric rub against the still raw love bites she'd bestowed earlier. I'd been much more discreet with Aurora's still unmarked flesh.

"I'll grill some patties," she said as she slipped effortlessly back into her cut offs and deftly twisted the scarf into a halter. "We use game meat mostly."

I followed her back into the great room and watched as she took meat patties from the freezer. They were soon sizzling on the oven top grill, spitting fat and smelling terrific. Wild boar, maybe, definitely not venison. Aurora cut thick slices of bread, her muscles bunching and rippling with the simple action, and I felt myself grow hard. This, I reminded myself, was not the time to appear lusty; he might walk in any minute. I went back to look at the mounted heads.

The glint of gold again caught my eye. I pushed aside the coral and picked up the locket, still attached to the thin gold chain I'd put on it, ten years ago. The chill that ran through me would have been welcome earlier today. Underneath was something else I recognized. Ned Barnes's

new cigarette case — the one he proudly flashed every time he took a cigarette and which he acquired just before we figured he eloped with Mrs. Clifton. I pushed it aside and saw things I didn't recognize, like a gold-trimmed fountain pen and a fancy cigarette lighter. Then it hit me. These weren't trinkets from anyplace far off and mysterious. They were souvenirs from Ridgeton.

A screech from outside, the same sound I'd heard this morning, rang through the room. Turning to the glass doors, any apprehension I'd felt before was replaced by absolute fear. At the edge of the small lawn a huge animal plodded wearily toward the house. Its massive head, framed by a magnificent black mane, hung low, and its loose-limbed floppy gait swayed rhythmically. It crossed the short expanse in seconds.

Stopping at the glass doors, which were just wide enough to admit its shoulder breadth, the monstrous cat paused and sniffed. A growl started low in its throat, building to that now familiar shattering roar.

I turned to the kitchen area, thinking of Aurora, alone in woods where animals not of this continent roamed, and saw her looking toward the door, her face radiating purest love.

"Darling, you're home," she purred. Then, glancing my way, her smile bypassed my loins this time and, instead, settled in my churning gut. She walked to the great beast and buried her head in the animal's glorious mane. With her arms still around the massive neck, and shaking her own mane of hair, she softly spoke to it, just loud enough for me to hear.

"If you're hunting wasn't good, dearest, mine was." 🕷

✍ Jean Paiva (1944–1989) had many careers: corporate communications, cable TV marketer, trade journalist, cofounder and editor of Crawdaddy magazine, and fantasy writer. NAL Onyx published two novels by Jean, The Lilith Factor and The Last Gamble. Only one short story was published during her tragically brief life, "Just Idle Chatter," in Kathryn Ptacek's Women of Darkness II, but she left nearly a dozen complete short stories behind, and this magazine is committed to printing them all. "Had she lived, she would have been one of the great dark fantasists," Tanith Lee writes.

I, WHO AM NOTHING
by Chris Bunch

There was a time, when I was a boy, when no sounds came to alarm me.

All was quiet, except for the birds, and the dull lowing of the oxen, my father's call from the field, or my mother's and sisters' chatter.

There was a war in our country, but the fighting was far distant. Occasionally young men with rifles came through, and we fed them and gave them shelter, but my father said that was because all travelers must be shown hospitality. Once in a while, one of our youths went with them when they left, and there was great lamentation.

I don't know how old I was when everything changed, but all else still comes most clear.

There was a strange roar one morning, and great air machines I'd only seen flying far overhead came down on us like locusts.

Then there was the chatter of machine guns and rifles, and the howls of the villagers as they died.

Soldiers came out of the machines, and commenced their killing.

A bullet struck me in the leg, and I fell.

Nothing swallowed me from the first time.

I came back to the screams, recognized them for my sisters', didn't want to open my eyes, but did, and saw the line of laughing troops, my youngest sister lying beneath them, another sister lying sprawled, a bayoneted rifle through her back.

One of the soldiers saw me move, came toward me, saying something I did not, must not, hear.

He was unbuttoning his trousers, and I felt the pain, the death, washing from him.

Somehow I reached out, took that death, and wrapped it around him like a cloak, as if he were one of our elders.

He screamed, writhed, and threw up his arms.

Then he fell.

The soldiers forgot about what they had been pleasuring themselves with, and ran to him.

But he was dead.

In their excitement, I crawled away, into a hay rick.

Again, nothing took me, and when I came back, there was no life in my village. Nothing. Not man, not beast.

The soldiers had gone.

I lay there, praying for that nothing to return.

But it did not.

After a time, I got up, dragged the torn bodies of my family into a pile, and fired them with oil.

Then I tied clothes around my wound, and hobbled away from what had been the only home I knew.

Eventually my leg healed, although I still could not run, could not walk like a normal boy. But boyhood lay behind me.

All that remained was the road. Sometimes I heard the helicopters, or tanks, and hid until the soldiers passed.

I tried to sleep as much as I could, for then came the nothing.

I had dreamed before, in my village, but dreamed no longer.

I fell in with some other wanderers, and one night, one of them came to me, before I fell asleep, wrapped in my rags.

I felt evil again in him, but a different, more deadly evil than the soldier had intended.

It was easy for me to take that evil from him, a swirling mist, and wrap it around his neck tightly.

He gargled, and was dead.

I did not want to explain to the others, so took what little I had, and crept away.

Then the soldiers were gone for a time, and I felt no evil. I tried to relax, but something said to embrace that nothingness that held me safe.

Then other soldiers came, and everyone waited for them to behave like the others.

Or, to be honest, like the men from our lands who came out from hiding, carrying guns, taking what they wished.

The soldiers said they intended peace, but our men didn't believe them.

I tried to pay no attention.

There was a school, and a schoolteacher who taught me to read, and to figure.

I did not want to. All I wanted was to be left alone, hidden in my nothingness.

But she would not let me.

So all I could do was what she wanted, and dream of that white nothingness, like snow on the distant mountain peaks, but swallowing all.

Something happened somewhere. I suppose some of these new warriors were killed, by our men who claimed they wanted peace.

Then the new soldiers began killing.

But not like the others.

They used machinery in the air, and along the

coast of my country, to kill from afar.

One day, one of these air-machines came, and, I don't know why, dropped bombs on my school.

The teacher and most of the students were killed.

But I was unharmed.

I took from their deaths a greater nothing, and could hide in it, needing nothing, not food, not water. No one could see me when I wore this cloak, or tent, or what it was, or at least they never paid me mind.

My cloak kept slipping, and I wanted vengeance for the deaths that followed me.

A column of tanks came to the village, painted in peaceful colors, and with men and women who cried over our dead. But they still wore uniforms and carried guns.

I waited until their column, a mercy column they called it, left the small town.

I was waiting, hidden, on the outskirts.

Now I took all the deaths, and coiled them like a striking snake, wrapping it around the growling steel tanks.

I heard screams, and saw the tanks going off the road, out of control. Then they stopped.

After a while, there were no screams, and the reward of nothing came to me.

I was walking away from that town, the road empty ahead and behind me, and I heard a dull rumbling.

I ran off the road, and crouched near the base of a dying tree.

I saw nothing, but the sound came more loudly.

Then I knew it for what it was — far, far overhead swam air machines.

I could feel the death they carried, but knew not where it would be dealt.

I was strong from the deaths of the men and women in the tanks, and found I could reach up, toward the air machines.

The deaths they carried were in bullets like the others, but also in pointed tubes, bigger than a man.

I could not understand how they worked, but could wrap around them, and bid them work as their makers had designed.

Far, far overhead came the waves of shock, and greasy fires flared for an instant, then bits of metal and flesh rained down.

Again, my blanket of nothing grew, and I could feel my own strength.

I didn't have to run any more.

Now there was more shooting, more of the air machines swooping overhead.

They came from great water-machines, ships not like the ones my father had carved, and set free down the brooks of our valley to run toward that sea.

These were huge, each of the big ones carrying more men and women than even the two cities I'd seen, and been afraid to enter.

And they carried death with them.

Some like the deaths I'd known.

But there was another kind.

This was a different kind of death, though, a death that embraced my nothingness, that was made of tiny particles of the earth, the sea, the air.

The men were afraid of these things, and kept them guarded and locked away, and, I felt, prayed they would never have to use them.

Their prayers meant nothing to me.

I felt one with these new devices, and walked among them, although no one could see me.

I felt these weapons' eagerness, and so caressed them with my mind, helped them reach their release.

Far out at sea, almost beyond the reach of my eyes, three monstrous fireballs came, and soared up toward the skies, leaving a trail of smoke and fire behind them.

The blasts caused waves that roared toward me, and I went higher in the hills as they approached.

Then there was nothing again, not just my nothingness, but an emptiness on the seas, where the ships had been and sunk. There was great death.

And the blanket grew stronger, and for the first time, I almost felt happiness.

But that would destroy my nothingness, and so I refused it, and turned it away.

There was great rejoicing in my land after the ships were destroyed, but I paid no attention to it.

My mind was reaching out, in other lands, and finding more of those weapons of nothingness, of the ultimate death, and noting where they were.

Some were on great pointed cylinders, some were like the cases I'd seen in the air machines, some, strangely enough, hiding under the seas.

I wanted to give them release, but kept my control until I had found a hundred hundred of them.

Now I can rest, knowing that sometime, this day, the next or the one after, I can reach out to these devices, and command them.

Then nothing can embrace us all. 🕷

✍ When not frothing at the mouth in Righteous Rage, Bunch works on the continuing Star Risk, Ltd., series for ROC and finishing up the Dragonmaster trilogy for Orbit.

WHERE DOES THE TOWN GO AT NIGHT?

by Tanith Lee

illustrated by Allen Koszowski

"Where does the town go at night?"

"What did you say?"

Gregeris turned, but some sort of vagrant stood there, grinning at him out of a dirty, flapping overcoat. Gregeris supposed he wanted money. Otherwise the broad square was deserted in the pale grey afternoon, its clean lines undisturbed by the occasional wind-breath from the sea which hardly even moved the clipped oleanders behind their prison-railings or the ball-shaped evergreens on long bare stems (like lollipops) which flanked most of the municipal buildings.

"Perhaps this will help?" Gregeris handed the man, the supposed beggar, a bank note. It was a cheerful, highly-coloured currency, and the man took it, but his smile lessened at once.

"I can't show you. You'll have to see for yourself."

"Oh, that will be all right. Don't trouble."

Gregeris turned to walk on. He had only come to the square to kill a little time, to look at the clock-tower, a sturdy thing from the 1700s. But it was smaller and much less interesting than the guide-book promised.

"Don't believe me, do you?"

Gregeris didn't answer. He walked firmly, not too briskly. His heart sank as he heard the scuffy footsteps fall in with his. He could smell the man too, that odd fried smell of ever-unwashed mortal flesh, and the musty dead-rat odour of unchangeable clothes.

"Y'see," said the beggar, in his low rough voice, "I've seen it happen. Not the only one, mind. But the only one remembers, or knows it isn't a dream. I've seen *proof*. Her, then, sitting there, right there, where the plinth is for the old statue they carted away."

There seemed nothing else for it. "The statue of King Christen, do you mean? Over there by the town hall?"

"The very one. The statue struck by lightning, and fell off."

"So I believe."

"But *she* was on the plinth. Much prettier than an old iron king."

"I'm sure she was."

The beggar laughed throatily "Still don't believe what I'm saying, do you? Think I'm daft."

A flash of irritation, quite out of place, went through Gregeris. It was for him an irritating time, this, all of it, and being here in this provincial nowhere. "I don't know what you *are* saying, since you haven't said." And he turned to face the beggar with what Gregeris would himself only have described as *insolence.* Because facing up to one's presumed inferiors was the most dangerous of all impertinences. Who knew what this bone-and-rag bag had once been? He might have been some great artist or actor, some aristocrat of the Creative Classes, or some purely good man, tumbled by fate to the gutter, someone worthy of respect and help, which Gregeris, his own annoying life to live, had no intention of offering.

And, "Ah," said the beggar, squaring up to him.

Gregeris saw, he thought, nothing fine or stricken in the beggar. It was a greedy, cunning face, without an actor's facial muscles. The eyes were small and sharp, the hands spatulate, lacking the noble scars of any trade, shipbuilding, writing, work of any sort.

"Well," said Gregeris.

"Yes," said the beggar. "But if you buy me a drink I'll tell you."

"You can buy yourself a drink and a meal with the money I just gave you."

"So I can. But I'll eat and drink alone. Your loss."

"Why do you want my company?" demanded Gregeris, half angrily.

"Don't want it. Want to tell someone. You'll do. Bit of a look about you. Educated man. You'll be more flexible to it, I expect."

"Gullible, do you mean?" Gregeris saw the man had also been assessing him, and finding not much, apparently. Less than flattery, education, he sensed, in this case represented a silly adherence to books — clerkishness. Well, Gregeris had been a clerk, once. He had been many things. He felt himself glaring, but the beggar only grinned again. How to be rid of him?

Up in the sky, the fussy clock-tower sounded its clock. It was five, time to take an absinthe or cognac, or a cocktail even, if the town knew they had been invented. Why hadn't the ridiculous tower been struck by lightning instead of a statue under a third its height?

"Where do you go to drink?"

Some abysmal lair, no doubt.

But the beggar straightened and looked along the square, out to where there was a glimpse of the sky — grey-rimmed, sulk-blue sea. Then he pivoted and nodded at a side street of shops, where an awning protected a little café from the hiding sun.

"Cocho's."

"Then take a drink with me at Cocho's."

"That's very sportive of you," said the beggar. Abruptly he thrust out his filthy, scarless and ignoble hand. Gregeris would have to shake it, or there would, probably, be no further doings. Ignore the ignoble hand then, and escape.

Compelled by common politeness, the curse of the bourgeoisie, Gregeris gripped the hand. And when he did so, he changed his mind. The hand felt fat and strong and it was electric. Gregeris let go suddenly. His fingers tingled.

"Feel it, do you?"

"Static," said Gregeris calmly. "It's a stormy afternoon. I may have given you a bit of a shock. I do that sometimes, in this sort of weather."

The beggar cackled, wide-mouthed. His teeth, even the back ones, were still good. *Better,* Gregeris resentfully thought, *than my own.* "Name's Ercole," said the beggar. (*Hercules,* wouldn't you know it.) And then, surprisingly, or challengingly, "You don't have to give me yours."

"You can have my name. Anton Gregeris."

"Well, Anton" (of course, the bloody man would use the Christian name at once), "we'll go along to Cocho's. We'll drink, and I'll tell you. Then I've done my part. Everything it can expect of me."

This was all Marthe's fault, Gregeris reflected, as he sipped the spiced brandy. Ercole had ordered a beer, which could be made to last, Gregeris ominously thought, until — more ominous still — he watched Ercole gulp half the contents of the glass at once.

It was because of Marthe that Gregeris had been obliged to come here, to the dull little town by the sea. His first impression, other than the dullness, had been how clean and tidy the town was. The streets swept, the buildings so bleached and scrubbed, all the brass-plates polished. Just what Marthe would like, she admired order and cleanliness so much, although she had never been much good at maintaining them herself. Her poky flat in the city, crammed with useless and ugly "objets d'art," had stayed always undusted. Balls of fluff patrolled the carpets, the ashtrays spilled and the fireplace was normally full of the cold debris of some previous fire. He suspected she washed infrequently, too, when not expecting a visitor. The bathroom had that desolate air, the lavatory unwholesome, the bath green from the dripping tap. And the boy — the boy was the same, not like Marthe, but like the flat Marthe neglected.

"Thirsty," mumbled Ercole, presumably to explain his empty glass.

"Let me buy you another."

"That's nice. Not kind, of course. Not kind, are you? Just feel you have to be generous."

"That's right."

The waiter came. He didn't seem unduly upset that Ercole was sitting at the café table, stinking and degenerate. Of course, Gregeris had selected one of the places outside, under the awning. And there were few other patrons, two fat men eating early plates of fish, a couple flirting over their white drinks.

When the second beer arrived, Ercole sipped it and put it down. "Now I'll tell you."

"Yes, all right. I shall have to leave at six. I have an appointment."

So after all Marthe (the "appointment") would be his rescue. How very odd.

"You'll realize, I expect," said Ercole, "I don't have lodgings. I had a room, but then I didn't any more. Sometimes I sleep in the old stables up the hill. But there's a couple of horses there now, and they don't like me about. So I find a corner, here or there. That's how I saw it. Then again, y'see, I might have been the type to just sleep right through it, like most of them. It's what's in you, if you ask me, in yourself, that makes you wake in the night, about a quarter past midnight."

"And what have you seen?" Gregeris heard himself prompt, dutifully.

Ercole smiled. He put his hands on the table, as if he wanted to keep them in sight, keep an eye on them, as if they might get up to something otherwise, while he revealed his secret.

"The town goes away."

"You mean it disappears?"

"Nothing so simple, Anton. No, it goes off. I mean, it *travels*."

Generally, I wake at dawn, first light, *said Ercole*. Like a damned squirrel, or a bird. Been like that for years. Sleeping rough's part of it, but I grew up on a farm. It's partly that, too. Well, when I woke the first time, which was about two months ago, I think it's dawn. But no, it's one of those glass-clear, ink-black summer nights. The moon wasn't up yet, but the stars were bright, and along the esplanade the street lamps were burning cold greeny-white from the funny electricity they get here. Nothing to wake me, either, that I can hear or see.

The moment I'm awake, I'm *wide* awake, the sort of awake when you know you won't sleep again, at least not for two or three hours, and it's better to get up and do something or you get to thinking. So presently I stand up. And then, well, I staggered. Which scared me. I hadn't had anything in the way of alcohol for about five days, so it wasn't drinking bad wine. And you can't afford to get sick, in my situation. But then my head cleared, and I just thought, maybe I got up too quick. Not so young as I was.

And then I go and take a stroll along the esplanade, like the leisured people do by day, which is when a policeman will generally come to move me elsewhere, if *I* try it. But no one's about now.

The sea is kicking away at the land, blue-black. It looks rough and choppy, which strikes me as strange really, because the night is dead calm, not a cloud. A sort of steady soft *thin* breeze is blowing full in my face from the mouth of sea and sky. It has a different smell, fresher, more starry *bright*.

When I looked over, down to the beach, the sea was slopping in right across it. It wasn't the tide coming in, I've seen plenty of those. No, the sea wasn't coming in, falling back but constant, gushing in up the beach, hitting the lower terrace of the esplanade, and spraying to both sides. Drops hit my face. It reminded me of something, couldn't think what. It looked peculiar, too, but I thought, after all tonight was a full moon and this moon would rise soon, maybe it was that making the sea act crazy.

Just then, the clock strikes on the tower in the square. It's one in the morning, and I can tell I've been up and about for around three quarters of an hour. That means I woke at a quarter past midnight.

I mention this, because another time I was in the square and when I woke, I noted the clock. It's always been that time, I reckon, that I wake, and the other ones who wake, they wake up then too.

That minute, the first night on the esplanade, I see one of my fellow awakers — only I didn't know it then, that we were a sort of select club. No, I thought there was going to be trouble.

It's a girl, you see, young, about sixteen, a slip of a thing, all flowing pale hair, and she's in her nightwear — barefoot — walking slowly along the esplanade towards me. Her eyes look like veiled mirrors, and I think she's sleepwalking or gone mad, and going to throw herself into the sea, and I'm asking myself if I should save her or let her do what she wants — have you got any more right to force someone to live that doesn't want to than to kill someone? — or if I'd better just hide, because trouble isn't what it's best for me to seek out, I'm sure you'll understand. Anyway, then she blinks, and she walks up to me and she says, "Where am I? What am I doing here?" And then I'm really scared, because she'll start screaming and God known what'll happen then. But next she says, "Oh but of course, that doesn't matter." And she leans on the railing and looks out at the sea, calm as you please.

The moon started to rise then. First a line like spilt milk on the horizon's edge. Then the sky turns light navy blue and the disc comes up so fast it almost seems to leap out of the water.

"I was in bed, wasn't I?" says the girl.

"Don't ask me. You just came along."

"They call me Jitka," she says. And then she says, "I think I looked out of the window at home. I think I remember doing that. And the hill wasn't there. You know, the hill with the old palace on it."

I know the hill, because that's where the stables are, my bedchamber of old. That big hill, about half a mile inland. Where all the historic splendour of the town is, the mansions and great houses and overgrown gardens of cobwebby, bathung cedars. And then the slums start all round it, either side.

Gregeris mutters that he knows the area, he has his appointment near there.

Well, I say to this girl called Jitka, "You've been sleepwalking, haven't you? Best get back indoors."

"No, I don't think so," says Jitka. Not haughtily as you might expect, but kind of wistful. As if she's saying, Just let me stay up half an hour longer, Dadda. But I'm not her father, so I turn away prudently, before I start trying to see through her flimsy nightie, past the ribbons to the other pretty things inside.

Perhaps not very gallant to leave her there, but I didn't go so far, only about fifty yards, before I find another one. Another Awaker. This was a gentleman sitting on a bench. He's in his nightclothes too, but with a silk dressing-gown fastened over. "Good evening," he says, and I can tell you, by day he'd have crossed the street not to see me, let alone exchange a politeness. But I nod graciously, and when he doesn't say anything else, I walk on.

The esplanade runs for a mile, no doubt you

know that from that guide-book in your pocket. I amble along it, and after another few minutes, I see these two old ducks tottering towards me, hand in hand. He's about ninety if he's a day, and she's not much less. He's got on a flannel nightshirt, the sort grandfather would've had, and she's in an ancient thing all yellow lace. And they're happy as two kids out of school. We pass within a foot of each other, and she calls out to me, "Oh isn't it a lovely fine night? What a lovely trip. Do you think we'll reach China?" So I generously say, "I should think so, lady." And they're gone, and I go on, and then I stop dead. I stare out to sea, and then down below the terrace again at the water rushing constant up the beach. What I'm thinking is this: But that's just what it's like, the way the waves are and the whole ocean parting in front of us — it's like a *bow-wave* cutting up before a ship. A moving ship, sailing quite fast. But then I think, Ercole, you've got no business thinking that. And suddenly I feel dog tired. So I turn and go back to my place under the columns of the library building, where I'd been sleeping. I lie straight down and curl up and pull my coat, over my head. At first I'm stiff as a plank. Then I fall asleep. And asleep I can feel it, what I'd felt standing up when I thought I'd gone dizzy. It's the motion of a ship, you see. Not enough to make you queasy, just enough you need to get your sea-legs. Then I'm really asleep. I didn't wake again until dawn. Nothing up then, not at all. A street-sweeper, and a pony-cart with kindling, and then a girl with milk for the houses by the park. A couple of cats coming back from their prowl. Moon down, sun up, rose-pink and blushing after its bath in the sea. That's all.

Gregeris says, "A memorable dream."

S'what I thought. Course I did. You don't want to go nuts in my situation, either. They cart you off to the asylum first chance they can get.

No, I went and scrounged some breakfast at a place I know, well, to be truthful, a garbage-bin I know. Then I went for my usual constitutional round the town. It was by the church I found them.

"Found what?"

Ah, what indeed. Sea shells. Beautiful ones, a big white whorled horn that might have come from some fabled beast, and a green one, half transparent, and all these little striped red and coral ones. They were caught in a trail of seaweed up in the ivy on this wall. People passed, and if they looked, they thought they were flowers, I suppose, or a kid's expensive toy, maybe, thrown up there and lost.

"Perhaps they were."

It didn't happen again for seven days. I'd forgotten, or pretended I'd forgotten. And once when I went back to that church, the shells were gone. Someone braver or cleverer or more stupid and cowardly than me had taken them down.

Anyway, this particular evening, I *knew*. Knew it was going to be another Night. Another *Awake Night*. I'll tell you how I knew. I was at the Café Isabeau, to be honest round the back door, where the big woman sometimes leaves me something, only she hadn't, but I heard this conversation in the alley over the wall. There's a young man, and he's trying to get his girl to go with him into the closed public gardens, under the trees, for the usual reason, and she's saying maybe she will, maybe she won't, and then I keep thinking I know her little voice. And then he says to her, all angry, "Oh please yourself, Jitka." And then *she* says to him, "No, don't be angry. You know I would, only I think I ought to be home soon. It's going to be one of those nights when I have that peculiar dream I keep on having."

"Come and dream with me," he romantically burbles and I want to thump him on the head with one of the trash pails to shut him up, but anyway she goes on anyhow, the way a woman does, half the time — if you were to ask me, because they're so used to men not listening to them. "I keep dreaming it," she says. "Five times last month, and three the month before. I dream I'm walking in the town in my nightclothes."

"I'd like to see *that!*" exclaims big-mouth, but still she goes on, "And seven nights ago, at full moon, I dreamed it. And I knew I would, all the evening before, and I know now I will, tonight. I feel sort of excited — here, in my heart."

"I feel excited too," oozed clunk-lips, but she says, "You see, the town slips her moorings. She sails away. The town, that is, up as far as King Christen's Hill. I watched it, I think I did, drifting back, like the shore from a liner. And then we sail through the night and wonderful, wonderful things happen — but I can't remember what. Only, I have to go home now, you see. To get some sleep before I wake up. Or I'll be so tired in the morning after the dream."

After she stops, he gives her a speech, the predictable one about how there are plenty of more sophisticated girls only too glad to go in the park with him, lining up, they are. Then he walks off, and she sighs, but that's all.

By the time I got round into the alley, she was starting to walk away too, but hearing me, she glanced back. It was her all right, even in her smartish costume, with her hair all elaborate, I knew her like one of my own. But she looked startled — no recognition, mind. She didn't remember meeting *me*. Instead she speeds up and gets out of the alley quick as she can. I catch up to her on the pavement.

"What do you want? Go away!"

"There, there, Jitka. No offence."

"How do you know my name? You were spying on me and my young man!"

Then I realize, a bit late, what I could be letting myself in for, so I just whine has she any loose money she doesn't want — and she rummages in her purse and flings a couple of coins and gallops away.

But anyway, now I know tonight is one of those Nights.

In the end, I climbed over the municipal railings and got into the public gardens myself. There's an old shed in among the overgrown area that no one bothers with. Lovers avoid it, too; there are big spiders, and even snakes, so I'm told.

I went to sleep with no trouble. Woke and heard the clock striking in the square, and it was eleven. Then I thought I'd never get off, and if I didn't I might not Wake at the *right* time — but next thing I know I am waking up again and now there's a *silence*. By which I mean the sort of silence that has a personality of its own.

Scrambling out of the hut, I stand at the edge of the bushes, and I look straight up. The stars flash bright as the points of gramophone needles, playing the circling record of the world. And now, now I can *feel* the world *rocking*. Or, the town, rocking as it rides forward on the swell of the sea. And then I saw this thing. I just stood there and to me, Anton, it was the most beautiful thing I ever saw till then. It was like the winter festival at the farm, when I was a child, you know, Yule, when the log is brought in, and I can recall all the candles burning and little silver bells, and a girl dancing, dressed like a fairy. That was magical to me then. But this.

"What did you see?" Gregeris asked, tightly, almost painfully, coerced into grim fascination.

It was fish. Yes, fish. But they were in the *air*. Yes, Anton, I swear to you on my own life. They were wonderful fish, too, painted in all these colours, gold and scarlet, and puce, mauve and ice blue, and some of them tiny, like bees, and some large as a cat. I swear, Anton. And they were swimming about, in the air, round the stems of the trees, and through the branches, and all across the open space of the park, about five feet up in the air, or a little lower or higher. And then two or three came up to me. They stared at me with their eyes like orange jewels or green peppermints. They swam round me, and one, one was interested in me, kept rubbing his tail over my cheek or shoulder as he passed, so I put up my hand and stroked him. And, Anton, he was *wet*, wet and smooth as silk in a bath of rain. So I knew that somehow, now, we weren't only on the sea, but *in* the sea, maybe *under* the sea. Even though I could breathe the air. And I thought, That's how those shells got stranded up on the church wall.

Well, I stayed sitting there in the park, watching the swimming, stroking them, all night. And once a shark came by, black as coal. But it didn't come for me, or hurt the others. Some of them even played round it for a while. No one else came. I thought, Jitka will be sorry to have missed this, and I wondered if I ought to go and find her, I knew she wouldn't be scared of me now, and find those others I'd seen, the rich man and the two old sticks, and bring them here. But they'd probably seen it before, and anyway, there were other things going on, maybe, they were looking at.

I suppose I drifted off to sleep again, sitting on the ground. Suddenly I was blinking at a grey fish flying out of a pine tree and it was a pigeon, and the sun was up.

"What's that?" said Gregeris abruptly.

The clock in the square, striking six.

"I should leave, I have an appointment." Gregeris didn't move, except to beckon the waiter. He ordered another brandy, another beer.

"Go on."

After that Night, I've had three others. I've always known, either in the afternoon or in the evening, they were coming on. Like you know if you have an illness coming, or someone can feel a storm before it starts.

Only not oppressive like that. Like what the girl said, an *excitement*.

Only it's a sort of cool green echo in your chest. In your guts. It's like a scent that you love because it reminds you of something almost unbearably happy, only you can't remember *what*. It's like a bitter-sweet nostalgia for a memory you never had.

Oh, I've seen things, these Nights. Can't recall them all, that's a fact. But I keep more than the others. They think they dream it, you see, and I know it isn't a dream. We're Awake, and God knows there are precious few of us who do come Awake. Most of the town sleeps on, all those houses and flats, those apartments and corners and cubby-holes, all packed and stacked with

sleepers, blind and deaf to it. Those buildings become like graves. But not for us. I've only met ten others, there are a few more, I should think. A precious few, like I said.

Jitka and I danced under the full moon once. Nothing bad. She's like a daughter to me now. She even calls me Dadda, in her dream. That was the night I saw her. I do remember her. Never forget. Even when I die, I won't forget her.

"The woman who was on the plinth," said Gregeris, "where the statue was taken down?"

Oh but Anton, she wasn't a woman.

"You said 'She'."

So I did. It was the last Wake Night, when I woke up in the square. Something had made me do that, like it always seems to make me choose a different place to sleep, when I sense a night is coming. Full moon, like I said, already in the sky when I bedded down, just over there, under those cut trees that look like balls on sticks.

And when I woke and stood up, I was so used to it by then, the movement of the town sailing, and the smell of the sea and the wind of our passage — but then the scent of the ocean was stronger than before, and I turned and looked, across the square, to where the plinth stood. It was draped in purple, and it was *wet* purple, it poured, and ran along the square. It ran towards the sea, but then it vanished and there was just the *idea* — only the idea, mind — that the pavement might be *damp*. You see, she'd swum up from the sea, like the fish, through the air which is water those Nights, and she'd had to swim. She couldn't have walked. She was a mermaid.

Gregeris considered his drink.

I won't even swear to you now, Anton. You won't believe me. I wouldn't expect it. It doesn't matter. Y'see, Anton, truth isn't killed if you don't believe in it — that's just a popular theory put about by the non-believers.

"A mermaid, you said."

A mermaid.

She was very absolutely white, not *dead* white, but *live* white. *Moon* white. And her body had a sort of faint pale bluish freckling, like the moon does, only she wasn't harsh, like the moon, but soft and limpid. And her skin melted into the blue-silver scales of her tail. It was a strong tail, and the fork of the fins was strong. Vigorous. Her hair was strong too, it reminded me of the brush of a fox or a weasel or ermine — but it was a pale green-blonde, and it waved and coiled, and *moved* on its own, or it was stirring in the breeze-currents of the water-air. And it was like currents and breezes itself, a silvery bristly silky fur-wind of hair. Her face though was still, as if it was carved like a beautiful mask, and her great still eyes were night black. She had a coronet. She was naked. She had a woman's breasts, the nipples watercolour-rose like her mouth. But you couldn't desire her. Well, I couldn't. She was — like an angel, Anton.

You can't desire an angel. I've heard the old church fathers said the mermaid was supposed to represent lust and fornication. But she wasn't like that. She was holy.

The funniest thing is, I looked at her a while and then, as if I'd no need to linger, as if the marvellous was commonplace and easy, I just turned and went off for a stroll. And on the esplanade I met Jitka, and I said, "Did you see the mermaid?" and Jitka said, "Oh yes, I've seen her." It was like being gone to heaven and you say, Have you seen God today, and they answer, But of course, He's everywhere, here. Then we danced. I don't know a thing about Jitka, but her father's dead, I'd take a bet on that.

The rich man was a soldier, did I say? The old couple are in the hospital. I don't know how they get out, but maybe everyone that doesn't wake up just *can't* wake up. And they get strong those Nights, they told me. It's the cruise, they said, this bracing cruise on this liner that's sailing to the East, India or China or somesuch. And there's a little boy I see now and then. And a woman and her sister —

I do think some of them are beginning to cotton on it's not a dream. But that doesn't matter. Nor who we are, we precious few, we're nothing, there and then. We're simply *The Awake*.

Ercole had ceased to speak. They must have sat speechless, unmoving, Gregeris thought with slight dismay, for ten minutes or more.

"So you see a mermaid?" Gregeris asked now, businesslike.

"No. That was the last Night. I saw her that once. I haven't Woken since. Which means there hasn't been a Night. I don't think there has. Because I think, once you start, you go on Waking."

"You didn't speak to the mermaid. *Stroke* her."

"Come on, Anton. I wouldn't have dared. Would you? It would have been a bloody cheek. I could have dropped dead even, if I touched her. Think of the shock it would be, like sticking your hand on the sun."

"Take off thy shoes from thy feet, this ground is holy."

"Yes, exactly that, Anton. You have it. By the way, you know, don't you, why God says that, in the Bible? It's to *earth* you, in the presence of galvanic might. Otherwise you'd go up in smoke."

Gregeris rose.

"I must get on. I'll be late for my appointment." He put another of the cheerful notes on the table. "It was an interesting story. You told it well."

The beggar grinned up at him. His face was fat now, bloated by beer and talk, by importance, power.

"But, where does the town go to at night?" he repeated. "More to the point, *why* does the town come *back* at dawn?"

"Yes, a puzzle. Perhaps enquire, the next time."

Gregeris reached the awning's edge. Instinctively, perhaps, he glanced across the square at the plinth of King Christen's fallen statue. In his mind's eye, transparent as a ghost, he visualized the mermaid, reclining in the opal moonlight, relaxed and thoughtful, her living hair and flexing tail.

It was only as he turned and began to walk quickly inland, that Ercole called after him. "Anton! It's tonight."

The flat-house had been stylish in the 1700s, he thought, about the time of the heyday of the clock. Now it was grimy, the elegant cornices chipped and cracked and thick with dirt, and a smell of stale cabbage soup on the stairs.

He rang the bell of her apartment, and Marthe came at once. She confronted him, a thin woman who had been slender and young twelve years ago, her fair hair now too blonde, and mouth dabbed with a fierce red which had got on to her front teeth.

"You're so late. Why are you so late? Was the train delayed? I was worried. I have enough to worry about. I thought you weren't coming, thought you'd decided to abandon us completely. I suppose that would be more convenient, wouldn't it? I can't think why you said you'd come. You could just send me another money order. Or not bother. Why bother? It's only me, and him. What do we matter? I've been just pacing up and down. I kept looking out of the window. I got some ice earlier for the wine but it's melted. I smoked twenty cigarettes. I can't afford to do that. You know I can't."

"Good evening, Marthe," he said, with conscious irony.

To Gregeris it sounded heavy-handed, unnecessarily arrogant and obtuse. But she crumpled at once. Her face became anxious, pitiable and disgusting. How had it been he had ever — ? Even twelve years ago, when she was a girl and he a younger man and a fool.

"I'm sorry. Forgive me, Anton. It's my nerves. You know how I get. It was good of you to come."

"I'm sorry, too, to be so late. I met an old business acquaintance at the station, a coincidence, a nuisance, an old bore who insisted we have a drink. He kept me talking. And of course, I couldn't make too much of it, of being here, or anything about you."

"No, no, of course."

She led him in. The apartment wasn't so bad, better than her last — or could have been. Everywhere was mess and muddle. The fairground knickknacks, some clothes pushed under a sofa cushion. Stockings hung drying on a string before the open window, the ashtrays were as always. Twenty cigarettes? Surely a hundred at least. But there was the cheap white wine in its bucket of lukewarm water. And she had made her bed. She had said she gave the bedroom over to the boy.

"How is Kays?"

"Oh — you know. He's all right. I sent him for some cigarettes. Oh, he wanted to go out anyway. He'll be back in a minute. But — I know — you don't like him much."

"What nonsense, Marthe. Of course I like him. He's only a child."

Taking him by surprise, as she always did for some reason, when she flared up, she shrilled, "He's your *son,* Anton."

"I know it, Marthe. Why else am I here?"

And again, the shallow awful victory of her crumbling face.

Once he had sat down, on a threadbare seat, the glass of tepid vinegar in his hand, she perched on the arm of the sofa and they made small talk.

And why had he come here? The question was perfectly valid.

It would have been so much simpler to send her, as she said, a cheque. That too, of course, was draining, annoying. Keeping it quiet was sometimes quite difficult, too. He was generally amazed no one had ever found him out, or perhaps they had and didn't care. His brief liaison with this woman had lasted all of two weeks. Two months later, when she reappeared, he had known at once. It.was damnable. He had taken every precaution he could, to protect both of them from such an accident. He wondered if her pregnancy owed nothing to him at all, he was only a convenient dupe. The storytelling beggar, Ercole, had had him to rights, Gregeris thought, bourgeois politeness and the fear of a sordid little scandal. It was these which had made him set Marthe up in the first flat, made him pay her food bills and her medical expenses. And, once the child was born, had caused him to try to pay her off. But however much he awarded her, in the end, she must always come creeping back to him, pleading penury. Finally he began to pay her a monthly sum. But even that hadn't been the end of it. Every so often, she would send a frantic letter or telegram — and these, if ignored, had on two occasions persuaded Marthe to appear in person, once with the child (then a snivelling, snotty eight-year-old, clinging to her hand), in the doorway of Gregeris's mother's house, during her 60th birthday dinner.

That time Gregeris had considered having Marthe, and very likely the boy, murdered. Just as he had, for a split second, considered murdering her himself that day by the canal when she announced, "You've put me in the family way, Anton. Fixed me up, good and proper, and you're the only one can set me right. Oh, not an abortion. I won't have that. One of my friends died that way. No, I need you to look after me."

And probably, thought Gregeris now, sipping the dying (really unborn) wine, only bourgeois politeness and the fear of a scene, that which had passed Marthe off to his mother as an "employee," had also saved her neck.

"I'm sorry about the wine," she fawned. "Of course, I could have asked you to bring some, but I didn't like to" (now fawning, slipping seamlessly to accusation), "it would have been nicer than what *I* can afford, though, wouldn't it? I can see you don't like this one. It was better cold. If you'd come sooner."

Poor bitch, he thought. Can't I even spare her a few hours, some decent food and drink? She's got nothing, no resources, she can barely even read. And I need only do this, what? Once or twice a year . . . once or twice in all those days and nights. He glanced at her. She had washed and was not too badly dressed, her bleached hair at least well brushed. Somehow she had even got rid of the lipstick on her teeth.

"When the boy comes back, why don't I take you to dinner, Marthe?"

Oh God. She flushed, like a schoolgirl. Poor bitch, poor little bitch.

"Oh yes, Anton, that would be such fun . . . But I can't leave Kays."

"Well, bring Kays. He can eat dinner too, I sup-

WHERE DOES THE TOWN GO AT NIGHT?

pose?"

"Oh no, no, I don't think we should. He gets so restless. He's so — awkward. He might embarrass you." Gregeris raised his brows. Then he saw she wanted to be alone with him. Perhaps she had some dream of reunion, or even of love-making. She would be disappointed.

At this moment the door to the flat opened, and his son walked in.

My son. The only son, so far as he knew, that he had. Kays.

"Good evening, Kays. You seem well. How are you going on?"

"All right."

Marthe looked uncomfortable, but she didn't reprove or encourage the monosyllabic, mannerless little oaf. Come to think of it, her own social graces weren't so marvellous.

As usual at a loss with children, "How is your school?" Gregeris asked stiffly.

"Don't go."

"Don't you? You should. Learn what you can while you have the chance —" The wry platitudes stuck in Gregeris's throat. It was futile to bother. The boy looked now less sullen than — what was it? Patient. *Bored,* by God.

What was that quaint adjective Gregeris had thought of for the sea? *Sulk*-blue, that was it. The boy's eyes were *sulk*-grey. Nearly colourless. Pale uneven skin, he would get spotty later no doubt, and perhaps never lose it, greasy tangled hair and unclean clothes that probably smelled. The child would smell, that unwashed-dog odour of unbathed children, redolent of slums everywhere. Like the beggar . . .

Take this child to dinner? I *don't think I will.* The mother was bad enough, but in some gloomy ill-lit café it would be tolerable. But not the weedy, pasty, morose brat.

My son. Kays. *How can he be mine?* He looks nothing like me. Not even anything like Marthe.

(For a moment, Gregeris imagined the boy's life, the woman leaning on him, making him do her errands, one minute playing with his dirty hair — as now — then pushing him off — as *now.* Always surprising him by her sudden over-sentimental affections and abrupt irrational attacks — perhaps not always verbal, there was a yellowish bruise on his cheek. And the school was doubtless hopeless and the teachers stupid and perhaps also sadistic.)

This was the problem with coming to see her, them. *This,* this thinking about her, and about Kays. The town by the sea should have taken them far enough away from Gregeris. It had

required three hours for him to get here.

"Well, Kays." Gregeris stood over him.

The top of the child's crown reached the man's ribcage. The child's head was bowed, and raised for nothing. "Here, would you like this?" Another cheerful note. Too much, far too much — someone would think the boy had stolen it. "Your mother and I are going out for some air. A glass of wine."

And she chirruped, "Yes, Kays, I'll take you over to Fat Anna's."

After all the boy's head snapped up. In his clutch the lurid money blazed, and in his eyes something else took pallid fire.

"No."

"Oh yes. You like Fat Anna's."

"Don't want to."

"Don't be a baby, Kays. Fat Anna will give you pancakes."

"No, she doesn't. No, not now."

Held aside in a globe of distaste, Gregeris watched the venomous serpent rise in Marthe and glare out from her eyes. "You'll do as I say, d'you hear?" The voice lifted, thin and piercing as the doorbell. "Do as I say, or I'll —" Checking now, not to reveal herself as hard or spiteful, unfeminine, unpleasant, before the benefactor — "Be a good boy," tardy wheedling, and then her hand gripping on the thin arm, working in another, dark-then-fade-yellow bruise. "I don't see your Uncle Anton, except now and then. He's too busy —"

Kays was crying. Not very much, just a defeated dew of tears on the white cheeks. But he made no further protest, well lessoned in *this* school at least.

Later, in the restaurant, among the nearly clean tablecloths, the wax stains and smell of meat sauce, Marthe confessed, "Anna locks him in the small room, she has to, he runs away. But I have to have him protected, don't I, when I'm not there — ?"

Gregeris, who had helped escort the prisoner to the woman's tenement cave (in one of the nastier streets, behind King Christen's Hill), considered that perhaps Marthe was often out, often away, at night. Or, more likely, often had company in at night. (The boy shoved in the bedroom and warned not to leave it.) It had been a man's shirt pushed under the sofa cushion. What a curious article to leave behind. Had Gregeris been meant to notice it?

He had intended to return that night to the city. But when he got free of Marthe it was almost ten, and Gregeris felt he was exhausted. The dinner, naturally, had been a mistake. They had parted, she with false sobs, and acrimony, Gregeris restrained, starchy, and feeling old.

What on earth had they said to each other? (Her excuse for demanding Gregeris's presence had been some conceivably-invented concern over Kays, that he slept poorly or something like that. But presently she said that he often ran away, even at night. And then again she said that she thought Kays was insane — but this was after the second bottle was opened.)

Otherwise, the conversation had been a dreary complaining recital of her burdensome life, leaving out, as he now thought, her casual encounters with other men, her possible prostitution. When at last he had been able to pay the bill and put her in a taxi-cab for the flathouse, her face was for an instant full of dangerous outrage. Yes, she had expected more. Was *used* to more.

After this, surely, he must keep away from her. During the meal, watching her scrawny throat swallowing, he had again wondered, with the fascination of the dreamer who could only ever fantasize, how much of a challenge it would be to his hands.

He found quite a good hotel, or his taxi found it for him, on the tree-massed upper slope of the hill. It nestled among the historic mansions, a mansion once itself, comfortable and accommodating for anyone who might afford it. Thank God for money and hypocrisy, and all those worthless things which provided the only safety in existence. He must never visit Marthe again. Or the awful boy, who surely could now only grow up to be a thug, or the occupant of some grave.

Gregeris took a hot bath and drank the tisane the hotel's housekeeper had personally made for him. He climbed into the comfortable, creaking bed. Sleep came at once. Thank God too for such sleep, obedient as any servant.

Gregeris woke with a start. He heard a clock striking, a narrow wire of notes. Was it midnight? Why should that matter to him?

He sat up, wide awake, full of a sensation of anxiety, almost terror — and excitement. For a moment he couldn't bring himself to switch on the lamp. But when he did so, his watch on the bedside table showed only eleven. He had slept for less than a quarter of an hour, yet it had seemed an eternity. The confounded clock in the square had woken him. How had he heard it, so far up here, so far away sound had risen, he supposed.

In any case, it was the beggar, that scavenger Ercole, with his tales of midnight and the town and the sea, who had caused Gregeris's frisson of nerves.

Gregeris drank some mineral water. Then he got up and walked over to the window, drawing back the curtains. The town lay below, there it was, stretching down away from the hill to the flat plain of the sea. There were fewer lights, all of them low and dim behind their blinds, only the street lamps burning white, greenish-white, as Ercole had said. The clock-tower, the square, were hidden behind other buildings.

When did the town, that part of the town beyond the hill, which went sailing, set off? Midnight, Gregeris deduced. That would be it. And so the motion would gradually wake those ones who did wake, by about a quarter past. After all, that hour, between midnight and one in the morning, was the rogue hour, the hour when time stopped and began again, namelessly, like a baby between its birth and its first birthday — not yet fully realized, or part of the concrete world.

It was quite plausible, the story. Yes, looking down from the hill at the town, you could credit this was the exact area which would gently unhook itself, like one piece of a jigsaw, from the rest, and slip quietly out on the tide.

Gregeris drank more water. He lit a cigarette, next arranged a chair by the window. Before he sat down, he put out his bedside lamp, so that he could see better what the town got up to.

This was, of course, preposterous, and he speculated if months in the future he would have the spirit to tell anyone, some business crony, his elderly mother, jokingly of course, how he had sat up to watch, keep sentinel over the roving town which sailed away on certain nights not always of the full moon, returning like a prowling cat with the dawn.

"A beggar told me. Quite a clever chap, rough, but with a vivid, arresting use of words."

But why had Ercole told him anything? Just for money? *Then I've done my part,* he had said. *Everything it can expect of me.*

It? Who? The town? Why did the town want its secret told? To boast? Perhaps to *warn.*

Gregeris gazed down. There below, hidden by the lush curve of the many-gardened hill, the slum where she lived, Marthe. And the boy.

There they would be, sleeping in their fur. And the town, sailing out, would carry them sleeping with it.

Gregeris couldn't deny he liked the idea of it, the notion of this penance of his carried far out to sea.

Well. He could watch, see if it was. Half amused at himself, yet he was strangely tingling, as if he felt the electricity in the air which had galvanized Ercole's filthy palm, and, come to think of it, the boy's, for when Gregeris had put the bank note into Kays's fingers, there had been a flicker of it, too, though none on Marthe. *Certainly I never felt more wide awake.*

He would be sorry, no doubt, in the morning. Perhaps he could doze on the train, although he disliked doing that.

It was better than lying in bed, anyway, fretting at insomnia. Avidly Gregeris leaned forward, his chin on his hand.

The sound was terrible, how terrible it was. What in God's name was it? Some memory, caught in the dream oh, yes, he remembered now, after that train crash in the mountains, and the street below his room full of people crying and calling, and women screaming, and the rumble of the ambulances —

Horrible. He must wake up, get away.

Gregeris opened his eyes and winced at the blinding light of early day, the sun exploding full in the window over a vast sea like smashed diamonds.

But the sound — it was still there — it was all round him. There must have been some awful calamity, some disaster — Gregeris jumped to his feet, knocking over as he did so the little table, the bottle and glass, which fell with a crash. Had a war been declared? There had been no likelihood of such a thing, surely.

Under Gregeris's window, three storeys down (as in the comfortable hotel all about), voices rose in a wash of dread, and a woman was crying hysterically, *"Jacob — Jacob —"*

Then, standing up, he saw. That is, he no longer saw. For the sight he would see had vanished, while he slept, he that had determined to watch all night, the sight which had been there below. The view of the town.

The town was gone. All that lay beyond the base of the hill was a great curving bay of glittering, prancing, sun-dazzled sea. The town had sailed away. The town had not returned.

Gregeris stood there with his hands up over his mouth, as if to keep in his own rash cry. *Marthe — Kays — The town had sailed away and they had*

been taken with it, for their slum below the hill was the last section of the jigsaw-piece, and they were now far off, who knew how far, or where, that place where those asleep slept on in the tombs of their houses (would they ever Wake? There was a chance of it now, one might think), and the air was sea, and fish swam through the trees and the creatures of the deeps, and the mermaid floated to the plinth, blue-white, white-blue-green, contemplative and black of eye — Someone knocked violently on the door. Then the door burst open. No less than the manager bounded into the room, incoherent and wild eyed.*

"So sorry to disturb — ah, you've seen, an earthquake, they say — the police insist we must evacuate — the hill's so near the edge — perhaps not safe — hurry, if you will — No! No time to throw on your coat — quickly! Oh my God, my God!"

Some big, ugly building accommodated the group in which Gregeris found himself. He thought it must be a school of some sort, once a grand house. It was cluttered with hard chairs, cracked windows, and cupboards full of textbooks. No one was allowed yet to leave. Everyone, it seemed, must give their name and address, even visitors such as Gregeris, and then be examined by a medical practitioner. But the examination was cursory — a light shined in the eyes, the tempo of the heart checked — and although three times different persons wrote down his details, still they refused to let him go. Soon, soon, they said. You must understand, we must be sure of who has survived, and if you are all quite well.

Several were not, of course. The fusty air of the school was thick with crying. So many of the people now crowded in there had "lost" — this being the very word they used — families, friends, lovers. Some had lost property, too.

"My little shop," one man kept wailing, blundering here and there. "Five years I've had it — opened every day at eight — where is it, I ask you?"

None of them knew where any of it was. They had woken from serene sleep to find — *nothing.* An omission.

It was an earthquake. That area had fallen into the sea. An earthquake and tidal wave which had disturbed no one, not even the pigeons on the roofs.

Had any others had a "warning," as Gregeris had? He pondered. Some of them, through their confusion and grief, looked almost shifty.

But his mind kept going away from this, the aftermath, to the beggar, Ercole. What had become of him, Awake, and sailing on and on? And those others, the girl called Jitka, the old couple from the hospital, and the rich soldier, and the ones Ercole hadn't met or hadn't recollected?

Was the town like one of those sea sprites in legend that seduced, giving magical favours and rides to its chosen victims, playing with them in the waves, until their trust was properly won. Then riding off deep into the sea and drowning them?

The thought came clearly. *Don't mislead yourself. It isn't that. Nothing so mundane or simple.*

God knew. Gregeris never would.

It was while he was walking about among the groups and huddles of people, trying to find an official who would finally pass him through the police in the grounds outside, that Gregeris received the worst shock of his life. Oh, decidedly the worst. Worse than that threat in his youth, or that financial fright seven years ago, worse than when Marthe had told him she was pregnant, or arrived in the birthday dinner door. Worse, much, much worse than this morning, standing up and seeing only ocean where the houses and the clock-tower and the square had been. For there, amid the clutter of mourning refugees from world's edge, stood Kays.

But was it Kays? Yes, yes. No other. A pale, fleshless, dirty little boy, his face tracked now by tears like scars, and crying on and on.

Some woman touched Gregeris's arm, making him start. "Poor mite. His mother's gone with the rest. Do you know him? Look, I think he knows *you*. Do go and speak to him. None of us can help."

And in the numbness of his shock, Gregeris found himself pushed mildly and inexorably on. A woman did, he thought, always manage to push you where she decided you must go. And now he and the boy stood face to face, looking up or down.

"How — are you here?" Gregeris heard himself blurt. And as he said it, knew. Fat Anna's street, where the boy had been penned, was the other, the wrong side, of the hill. And Marthe, damn her, drunk and selfish to the last, hadn't thought to fetch him back. Gregeris could just picture her, her self-justifying mumbles as she slithered into her sty of a bed. *He'll be all right. I'm too upset tonight. I'll go for him in the morning.*

Good God, but the boy had *known* — his panic, for panic it had been, his rage and mutiny that he

was too small to perpetrate against the overbearing adults. And that fat woman locking him up so he couldn't escape, as normally he always did from Marthe . . . Ercole had said, "And there's a little boy I see, now and then."

"You were *Awake,*" Gregeris said.

They stood alone in the midst of the grey fog, the misery of strangers.

"I mean, you were Awake, those special Nights. Weren't you, Kays?"

Sullen for a moment, unwilling. Then, "Yes," he replied.

"And so you knew it was a Night, and you wanted to be able to go with the town, to see the fish and the mermaid — to get *free.*"

Kays didn't say, How do you know? You, of all people, how can *you* know?

His face was so white it looked clean. It was clean, after all, clean of all the rubbish of life, through which somehow he had so courageously and savagely fought his way, and so reached the Wonder — only to lose it through the actions of a pair of selfish blind fools.

"Did you know — did you know this was the last chance, the last, Night?"

The boy had stopped crying for a minute. He said, "It could have been any Night. Any Night could have been the last chance."

Oh God, when we dead awaken — the last trump sounded and the gate of Paradise was flung wide — and we kept him from it. Just because we, she and I, and all the rest, have always missed our chance, or not, seen it, or turned from it, despising. She slept like a stone, but he, my son, he woke. And I've robbed him of it for ever.

"Kays . . ." Gregeris faltered.

The boy began to cry again, messily, excessively, but still staring up at Gregeris, as if through heavy rain.

He wasn't crying for Marthe, how could he be? But for Paradise, lost.

"I'm so sorry," said Gregeris. Such stupid words.

But the child, who saw Truth, his child, who was Awake, knew what Gregeris had actually said. He came to Gregeris and clung to him, ruining his coat, weeping, as if weeping for all the sleeping world, and Gregeris held him tight. 🕷

Tanith Lee, who prefers writing longhand with a pen, has won the August Derleth, Nebula, and World Fantasy awards. She lives on the English seacoast with her husband John Kaiine.

PIT OF MADNESS

by E. Hoffmann Price

Bayonne seemed incredibly ancient and lovely to Denis Crane as he headed from the wine shop on Biarritz Highway and across the sombre parkway toward the Gate of Spain. The cathedral spires were silver lance-heads reaching into the moonglow, and the city was a pearl gray enchantment afloat on a sea of writhing river mists: yet that blood soaked soil whispered to Denis Crane as he walked.

This was unholy ground, honey-combed with crypts in which Roman legionnaires had worshiped Mithra, and watched frenzied devotees slash and mutilate and emasculate themselves in honor of bloodthirsty Cybele. This corner of France was the home of witch and wizard and warlock.

A shiver rippled down Crane's lean, broad-shouldered body as he glanced to his left and saw the ominous cluster of ancient trees that overshadowed the low gray cupola of the spring where Satan and Saint Leon once had met —

Another medieval legend. Well, and here is the causeway, and just ahead, rue d'Espagne, with the yellow glow from the windows of Basque wine shops breaking its narrow gloom.

But the scream that came from his left told him how far from warm humanity he was, however near the lights might be. It was the sobbing, desperate outcry of some woman whose last gasp could not quite voice her terror.

Crane's suntan became a sickly yellow in that spectral, mist-filtered moonlight. He wheeled, stared into the swirling grayness of the dry moat that girdled the thirty-foot city wall. His face lengthened, tightened into grim angles, and his eyes narrowed as he listened. Silence — sinister . . . poisonous. . . . Then that dreadful wail again. It was closer now, and though it was inarticulate he knew that the woman was crying for help and despaired of getting it.

An everlasting instant, and she burst from the mist and into the foreground at the foot of the causeway that blocked the moat. Her abrupt appearance shocked Crane, though he knew that it was but the illusion of fog and moonlight.

Her hair was a streaming blackness, and her body a pearl-white glow. Her feet and legs were as bare as her torso. All she wore was a flimsy shawl caught at the shoulder, draping slantwise to veil one breast, and flaring out, to shroud the opposite hip. Crane distinguished no feature but her mouth. It was distorted in a cry she could not utter.

He plunged down the steep slope of the causeway and into the moat. Her legs gave way, pitching her headlong to the sand. She lay there, arms sprawled out. As he reached her side, she shuddered and slumped flat, no longer making instinctive efforts to protect herself.

Crane rolled her over into the crook of his arm. He saw then what mist and motion had masked: her throat was savagely torn, her breast and stomach clawed and lacerated. Her face was a gory crisscross of bruises and slashes. The filmy fragility of the shoulder-to-hip shawl had not hampered her assailant enough for him to tear it from her body.

Neither pulse nor breath was perceptible. Though her sweetly curved body was blood-splashed, her wounds could not have killed her; but terror and despair could have.

Her face must have been as lovely as her body; but horror blinded him to the sleekness of her hips and the shapeliness of her legs and firm young breasts. His eyes narrowed as he recovered sufficiently from the shock to interpret certain significant signs.

Her hands had the incredible softness of one utterly a stranger to the lightest work; but what she still clenched in her fingers was a startling revelation.

It was similar in shape to a military campaign badge: purple, with a rosette of the same color. A decoration awarded to an elect few.

But most revealing of all was the silken shawl. It placed her beyond any question. There was only one house in Bayonne where the girls paraded in such costume; and that place was on the street that ran along the city wall.

Then he noted that she was breathing; and a slash on her inside arm was bleeding. It might not be dangerous, but it was near an artery. He drew a clean handkerchief from his breast pocket, and devised a tourniquet.

The town was asleep, and he'd have to carry her to the house on the wall; but first give that tourniquet a twist. He fumbled for a pencil —

But Crane's first aid was not completed.

PIT OF MADNESS

The sand of the moat bottom gave no betraying crunch; the mist thinned moonlight cast no warning shadow; and Crane's intuition was an instant too late. He dropped the battered girl, but before he caught more than a fleeting glimpse of the dark figure which loomed monstrously above him in the grayness, a flying tackle carried him crashing to the ground.

The impact knocked him breathless. Iron hands clutched his throat; but Crane's fist hammered home. Splintered teeth lacerated his knuckles, and blood gushed, drenching his face. His opponent, snarling scarcely articulate curses, jerked back. Crane's boot lashed out.

But the moonlight was blocked by another figure with monstrous, outspread wings. Bat wings, it seemed. It dropped, boring headlong, toppling Crane backward. A spicy, pungent odor, an odd blend of incense and cosmetics stung his nostrils. Then, still grappling with the thing which

had swooped out of the upper mist, he crashed against the gray masonry of the bastioned wall.

Crane's hard head had not a chance against a fortress built to defy a battering ram, but his shoulders absorbed enough of the terrific impact to save his skull. Some lingering vestige of wits told him that once out of action, he no longer interested the enemy.

Minutes elapsed before he could fight off the numbness and inertia that clogged his will. But he finally rolled over and clambered to his knees.

He was alone in that gray, ghoulish moonglow. The girl was gone. He saw the prints of his own feet and those of the mysterious assailants that had swooped down on him. Blood flecked the sand, and one untrampled spot still held the imprint of that savagely slashed girl's breasts. It had not been illusion; but for a moment Crane's blood became ice.

The laundry marks and monogram on the

by E. Hoffmann Price

77

handkerchief he had bound to the girl's arm would damn him beyond redemption when her body was found. And aside from that, he could not hope to obliterate the traces of the struggle in the moat.

The French police, inhumanly efficient, would inevitably connect him with the outrage. When he returned to his quarters, the concierge would note the time of his arrival. The proprietor of the wine shop on the Biarritz Road would remember when he had left, and the direction he had taken. And every foreigner is conspicuous in sleepy Bayonne.

Damn those experts with their omniscient microscopes! Their chemical tests which would detect the faintest trace of blood on his clothing.

And someone, watching from some darkened window of a house on the wall, might observe him as he left the moat, might already have heard and noted the encounter.

Only one move for Crane: find that girl, dead or alive. Hit first before the merciless *Sûrete Générale* connected him with the work of night-roving ghouls. And find the man whose decoration she had clutched.

As he hastened down the moat, he followed the girl's small, shapely footprints along the sand. Wrath burned him as his first fear left. Though that gaudy shawl branded her, she was still a woman, and the victim of something monstrous and deadly; something too eager for her torn flesh to bother with Crane beyond hammering him out of action.

Or had the two spectral assailants already arranged to frame him?

Half way to the sombre Lachepaillet Gate he noted the spot where her bare feet first marked the moat-bottom sand. He entered the walled city and hastened to his room at the Panier-Fleuri. The concierge regarded him with bleary eyes that suddenly sharpened. But she said nothing.

Once in his room, he cleaned up, then stretched long legs toward rue Lachepaillet. He should report to the police; but who would believe such a story, told by an insane American, trying to implicate one who wore that coveted purple decoration the size of an A.E.F. campaign badge?

Crane jabbed a pushbutton. A trim, sharp-eyed girl in black admitted him and led the way to a spacious hall whose walls and ceiling were a solid expanse of mirror.

A bell tinkled, and a half a dozen girls lounging on upholstered benches lined up on parade as several others emerged from a rear apartment to join them.

They wore satin slippers and knee-length silk hosiery. Their professional smiles, and the flimsy chiffon shawls draped from right breast to left hip completed their costume. Not a bad array; though some had over-plump legs, and breasts that would have been the better for a brassiere. A few were lovely in face and body, but there was something infinitely repulsive about that grotesque multiplication of bare flesh in those mirrored panels whose angles probed the concealment of chiffon shawls and made the glaring room a patchwork of feminine curves.

Crane caught a freshly mirrored whiteness and turned toward the door. The shock for an instant numbed him. A full moment elapsed before he realized that he was not looking at the girl who had vanished from the moat.

She had the same gracious inward dip at the waist, the same heart-warming flare of the hips, and one lovely breast peeped alluringly through the heavy strands of hair that trailed down over her left shoulder. Her blue eyes were almost black. Their troubled darkness matched the sombre droop of her lips.

Tears had smudged the mascara of her lashes and a trace of redness lingered. Crane perceived the tensity of her body and saw her fingers twisting the trailing fringe of her shawl.

Why had she been reserved from the line-up? Why that startling resemblance to that savagely mutilated girl in the moat? Why that black fear in her eyes?

The girl's fingers sank insistently into his wrist, and he felt the firm pressure of her hip and shoulder against him as she paused in the doorway.

More than her resemblance to the girl in the moat told Crane that this was the one who could give him the most help — or damn him soonest. He followed his hunch.

"Allons!" he whispered. "Let's go."

He tossed the three-hundred-pound keeper of the house a purple Banque de France note, and followed the girl in the scarlet shawl up a flight of stairs and into a sombrely furnished room.

Her name was Madeline, but all the coquetry of the game was missing, though she contrived a friendly smile as her fingers plucked the shoulder knot of her shawl.

Crane checked her.

"What's wrong?" he demanded.

"Diane — my sister," she answered. "I'm terribly worried. She hasn't come back. That awful Arab — or Turk —"

Crane frowned. That was an odd touch. Who

ever heard of an Algerian wearing that decoration?

As she spoke, she abstractedly kicked off her slippers and leaned back among the cushions. She regarded Crane curiously, seeing that his face was gray and grim.

"What's the matter . . . don't you like me?"

"That will keep!" His voice was harsh and low. "Tell me about that Arab. What was wrong with him?"

"Some of the things he did, the first night he was here. Before he took Diane — wherever he's taken her. It was in the room next door. No, he didn't hurt her at all — I mean the other girl, not Diane. But he frightened her terribly. I saw him leave. His pupils were like black saucers. *Mon Dieu!* Such eyes. Like Satan eating opium."

She was wrong. Opium contracted the pupils, but her very intensity gave Crane the picture.

"Are you sure he didn't wear the Order of Saint Leon?"

"Mumm . . . no, of course not! But he dropped something in her room, and she showed it to me, and left it here." Madeline slid to her feet and stepped to the dresser. She returned with a small silver watch charm. It was a tiny peacock with ruby eyes; an exquisitely tooled bit of metal.

"A soldier who'd served in Syria once told me," explained Madeline. "That that is a symbol of the devil-worshipers. That's what's been worrying me. If I'd known in time, I'd never have let her go. But why should you care?"

"I'm a damn fool who can't mind his business," Crane smiled grimly. "I've got to find your sister." She skeptically eyed him.

"Then you don't want me? But you paid —"

Crane shrugged. "If you knew, you'd understand.

"Oh . . ." Very slowly, like a dying echo. She caught him by the shoulders, stared him full in the face; and bit by bit she read that the sombre riddle in his gray eyes concerned her missing sister.

"I didn't realize you knew Diane . . ." Her arm slipped about his neck and she drew closer as she continued, "I'll go with you. I'll help."

She had guts. Crane's smile lost his bleakness. For a long moment their glances blended. She sighed, and her breasts crept through their screen of dark curls. Her smile was a revelation, and suddenly Crane's blood quickened from the soft caress of her arm and the warmth of her body.

"*Tenez!*" protested Crane. "Stop it, you damn little fool. I've got some business to attend to —"

"You wouldn't buy me," she whispered. "Somehow, that's rather wonderful . . . but you like me just a little, don't you? Wouldn't that make it different?"

Somehow, it did; and Crane's sensible effort to break away failed. She was lonely and worried. He couldn't repulse her friendliness.

"Cut it out!" he growled, though his protest was weakening. He laughed harshly, thinking of the one about the mail-carrier who hiked on Sundays; but Madeline seemed no longer one of those who lined up in that mirrored hell-glare. She had become a bright flame in the foulness that crept through the mists of that fiend-haunted gray city.

Those were not bought lips that clung thirstily to Crane's mouth, and the shudder that rippled down her throbbing body was instinctive . . . and as her arms closed about him, Crane defied the peril that was gathering outside. He could not repulse the first glow of friendliness in that drab lupanar . . .

Madeline's eyes were tear-sparkling when she slipped from Crane's arms and said, "I know now that she is dead."

"The devil you do!" he snapped, feeling decidedly stupid about the interlude that might in the end cost him all but his head — literally, as they use the guillotine in France.

"Yes. Or you'd not have lingered, with that wrath in your eyes. So I know you can't find her alive."

No use explaining his true motives. He took a key from his pocket.

"Go to the Panier-Fleuri. Stay under cover. What you told me about an Arab has entirely upset my assumption. I thought you could tell me about someone wearing the Order of Saint Léon. But no matter — I've got a fresh hunch. Now run along."

They waited for the cessation of laughter and footsteps in the hall. A latch click. Silence, except metallic voices from the reception room on the ground floor.

Crane watched Madeline slip toward the further stairway. A moment later, looking from the window that overlooked the narrow black alley that skirted the rear of the house, he saw the white blur of her face, and caught the gesture of her hand.

She was on her way. He slammed the door and strode down the main stairway. He forced a laugh at the doorkeeper's vulgar farewell; but as he crossed the threshold, he began to see that his investigation, despite the delay, had gained him an ally if the police should catch up with him.

But that silver peacock was an ominous hint. Devil worship . . . some damnable Asiatic cult. He'd heard it existed in the mountains of Kurdistan.

Yet for all that thickening menace, the riddle in some respects was less baffling in the light of reflection.

Diane had been headed off by the monsters that had swooped down on Crane from the lip of the moat. They must have held to a straight line across the parkway. That gave him a start toward tracing the point from which she had made her futile break.

The mist was thinning, yet enough remained to envelop Crane in a spectral veil that protected and at the same time hampered him. He was unarmed; but he paused long enough to remove his socks, stuff one inside the other, and then slip in a rock the size of his fist. Very pleasant, if he got the edge on the two who had laid him out.

For half an hour he circled, trying to pick a course that the two monsters would have used to head off the mangled fugitive.

"Her instinct would drive her to the closest route to safety," he reasoned. "To her sister. Then, if the Gate of Spain was the closest, her direction must have been more to my left. Otherwise she'd have gone through the Lachepaillet Gate."

Half an hour search vindicated the hunch. A shred of scarlet chiffon. A splash of blood.

He looped left. He found footprints heading toward the Gate of Spain — her pursuers, eager to cut off a flight that would betray their rendezvous.

Ahead of him a masonry lunette loomed low in the mist. One of the outer defenses erected by Vauban — or perhaps something much more ancient, and conceived by no honest engineer.

Crane now crept through the mists until a whiff of stale tobacco warned him of a watcher's presence.

He rose and boldly stalked toward the lunette. A jet of light flared in his face, blinding him. He was challenged in French.

"I've got to see the *émir* at once!" Crane bluffed, using a plausible Arabic title that would flatter anyone of lower rank.

The sentry protested. The *émir* was not to be disturbed. The ceremony had started. Crane shrugged and offered him the silver peacock.

"Hurry, idiot!" growled Crane. "Tell him I'm here!"

The flash shifted toward the silver token. The drawn pistol was holstered and an empty hand reached for the symbol. And then Crane's bludgeon cracked down. The guardian collapsed. Crane caught him and the flashlight.

The fellow was wearing a gown, and a hood from which hung a mask to conceal his face. Crane donned the disguise. This was no time for qualms.

The memory of that mangled girl nerved his arm. He raised the pistol, smashed down with the barrel. Then he picked his way down a narrow casemate inclining sharply into the earth.

Furtive flashes of his light guided Crane. He descended a stairway of archaic masonry, crumbled treads whose rubbish litter had been swept against the walls. A splash of fresh blood guided him.

Finally there was an indirect glow ahead. Drums were thumping, and voices muttered in eerie rhythm. Some satanic ritual was in progress.

Reasonably, Crane should now notify the police; but that brained sentry left him with no retreat. More than ever, his story had to be good.

He halted at the jamb of an arch opening into a vaulted chamber illuminated by flickering wax tapers. Its circular walls were pierced with other arches that led to further and darker crypts.

Upward of a score of scarlet-robed and hooded figures were informally gathered in groups. They sat on low wooden tripods the size of coffee tables. Their muttered conversation was low-voiced and unintelligible, but Crane sensed the tension that gripped them, felt their awe and soul-stabbing anticipation.

There was one, tall and commanding, who strode from group to group. Red masked faces jerked abruptly upward at his approach.

But most revealing of all was the blank arch opposite Crane. Stretched out on a massive block of stone lay a woman, bound hand and foot: Diane, recaptured for the ritual from which she had escaped. Her body was to serve as an altar, perhaps to feel the thrust of a sacrificial knife. Black candles burned about her, diffusing acrid fumes which half obscured her; but Crane saw that she breathed. The tourniquet with his initials, however, had been removed.

Since Diane was alive, he need not find that damning handkerchief, provided that he could extricate her. But though he was armed with the sentry's pistol, the odds were far too great for open attack.

Then he saw that the figure on the two-foot, brazen crucifix behind that altar of bare, lacerated flesh was inverted. That final detail sent frost racing through his blood. Those hooded figures had gathered for the Black Mass, the evil rit-

ual of modern satanism, utterly different from the oriental devil-worship. Crane wondered how that silver peacock fitted into the tangle.

From one of the passages at the left came bestial snarls and half human mutterings: some monster held in reserve for the ultimate horror of that mad gathering.

The lordly figure in black clapped his hands. The devotees shifted into crescent formation. Crane joined them as they moved toward the altar.

The Black Monster was donning a priest's stole and cope. Six red-robed acolytes filed from a passageway. Three carried thuribles from which poured blue-black, pungent fumes; the others had trays of hammered copper, all heaped with diamond-shaped lozenges. They passed among the gathering, swinging their thuribles and offering wafers to the devotees.

Crane tasted one of the confections; but instead of swallowing, he palmed it. It reeked with hasheesh and datura, blended with other oriental drugs he could not identify; but the two he recognized warned him. Both were brain-searing aphrodisiacs. Those wafers of illusion would make the partaker a crazed beast gnawed by outrageous fancies and delusions. That would give Crane his chance to act.

And all the while that bestial mumbling and groaning and the vibration of pounded iron echoed from the further crypt.

Crane watched the high priest of Satan make a foul mockery of the genuflections of the Mass, saw him spit upon the reversed crucifix, heard him chanting in a high, malignant voice.

Crane could scarcely understand the ritual, but some phrases of ultimate blasphemy were all too clearly burned into his reeling brain.

"Satan, Lord of the World, defend us against an unjust god who created only to damn . . . defend us against hypocrisy that mocks with the lure of redemption . . . hear the voice of the damned, O Lucifer, Son of the Morning! Satan, to you we make our prayer, Just and Logical God . . . ."

Finally, the priest faced about and mocked the caricatured crucifix.

"And You, O Thief of Homage and Deceiver of Mankind, I compel you to become incarnate in this bread . . . by the mockery you have ordained, I who am ordained command you and you will obey . . . yea, while we draw blood anew from your wounds . . . and press fresh thorns of vengeance on your brow . . . this I can and this I will do . . . Accursed Nazarene . . . Traitor Son of a Traitor God . . ."

A low rumbling mutter drowned his amen; then

with an inverse gesture of his left hand, the priest blessed the gathering and in mocking accents completed the blasphemy: *"Hoc est enim corpus meum!"*

He spat upon the consecrated bread, stolen from some consecrated altar; he scattered the fragments among the frothing, slavering devotees. They closed in, maddened with blasphemy and Asiatic drugs. They groveled, clawing and growling as they fought for the fragments.

Crane joined them. It was too early for a break. He had to outwit the un-drugged acolytes.

First voices, then the tearing of the scarlet robes told him that women were among those who writhed and panted and grappled on the floor. Hoods and masks yielded to clawing fingers. Soon they forgot blasphemy. The Asiatic drugs were biting deep.

In a moment the vault had become an animation of the bestial carvings of a Tantric temple. Women in jewels and costly gowns, and men in formal evening dress were clawing each other with a fury that stripped clothing to shreds.

A golden-haired fiend with crazed eyes and hungry red mouth emerged unpaired from the tangle and twined eager arms about Crane. A few scraps that glittered with green sequins trailed from her hips and what remained of a brassiere clung to breasts that throbbed from her fierce, drugged passion. Her legs were white serpents and her quivering body was a multitude of consuming flames, and her loose hair blinded and choked Crane as he swallowed his horror of that uncontrollable madness.

Yet he had to play his part. That black-robed demon's eyes glittered fiercely from behind his mask as he circled the arena, watching their ever fouler fancies cropping out . . .

That golden-haired woman's madness was cleaner than what was on every side. And despite his qualms, Crane's blood surged in irrepressible response to her savage frenzy . . .

Yet even as he yielded to that vortex of passion, a remote corner of his brain remained untainted. He plied her with answering kisses, felt the shudder of her hot flesh, but that one sane morsel was wondering. And at times he saw what was about him.

He recognized a black-bearded man whose face had appeared in every major newspaper of the world . . . another, who had led a victorious army . . . and one who from the sidelines told premiers what to say . . .

The Master gestured, and an acolyte dashed to the passageway at the left.

Crane's fist smashed home, driving away a black-haired woman who sought to displace his companion. Her body was raked and bitten and slashed, but she was seeking more savage company . . . Crane saw how Diane had been mangled. Her terror hinted that she had not been drugged . . .

Then Crane saw what had been released when those unseen iron bars clanged open. A tall, gray-haired man whose deeply-lined face had once been handsome and commanding. He wore what remained of full evening dress. The ribbon that had crossed his shirtfront trailed like a streamer as he approached; and on it Crane saw the ribbons of civil and military decorations.

He recognized the man. He knew now from whose formal garb that purple rosette had been torn. His mouth frothed, and his eyes burned insanely. He snarled bestially and plunged into

the surging orgy.

This was a man whose whispers shook Europe. Now he rolled vilely in that tangle of writhing flesh.

But why — Great God, why?

The Master laughed and gestured. The sullen ruddy glow of the tapers was drowned in a blue white, dazzling radiance, pitilessly revealing what shadows had shrouded.

Then Crane saw and understood.

A motion picture camera was covering the hideous show. That damnable film would place those drugged dignitaries forever in the power of that master of blasphemy. He had tricked them from Biarritz with hints of sensational ritual, drugged them, and the record of their unspeakable wallowings would doom them. Satanism had a logical purpose — political blackmail.

Time to move. The Master was distracted by his own show. Crane kicked clear of his companion, reached for his pistol.

It was gone! Lost in that writhing vortex.

He bounded to the altar, snatched that mockery of a crucifix, and whirled toward the Master. A pistol crackled. Crane felt the stab of hot lead, hurled himself aside as bullets spattered the masonry. The acolytes closed in. The brazen crucifix crunched home. But the survivors overwhelmed him, hammering and kicking and grinding him into the flagstones.

The Master joined them. Crane, battered and stunned, heaved up out of the gory tangle, clawed the mask aside. He slashed at that swarthy, aquiline face. He missed, ducked a knife thrust, and closed in. This was the *émir*, the Asiatic enemy whose grip on the drugged dignitaries would buy state and army secrets, upset an African colonial empire.

Crane bored in, but the enemy was fresh and he was dizzy and battered. They crashed to the floor, Crane underneath, vainly trying to drive home one good blow. He jerked clear of a second knife thrust; but the next raked his ribs. The vault became a roaring redness until he perceived nothing but those implacable eyes and that savage, brazen leer.

But that last stroke did not fall. The surging tangle of madmen, sated of all but blood lust, swept Crane and his enemies against the wall. As the acolytes strove to club them into reason, Crane made the most of his respite.

He snatched an abandoned thurible by the chains, swung it like a flail, flattening the Master's skull. He swung again, but the chains whipped athwart a devotee who intervened, and the weapon was jerked from Crane's grasp. He

turned toward the altar, ploughing through the writhing tangle. He tripped and was dragged back into the whirlpool of madness, a yard short of his goal.

A pistol roared as he struggled to his feet.

Madeline had followed him.

Crane jerked the weapon from her fingers and blasted the acolytes back as she struggled with her sister's bonds.

Another shot. The cameraman toppled from his perch behind the altar. The pistol was empty. Crane seized the machine and smashed it across the head of a surviving enemy. The film reservoir spewed out its reel of yellow celluloid, fogged beyond redemption in an instant.

The knots yielded. Crane seized the half-conscious girl and with Madeline at his heels, skirted the groveling tangle of drugged devil-worshipers. There were no acolytes left to pursue. And presently they reached the mist and moonlight . . .

"As you learned," explained Diane, hours later, in Crane's rooms, "I was just frightened helpless by your dashing down to meet me. The *émir* didn't intend for me to be clawed to ribbons. But *Monsieur le Général* Mar —"

"Forget his name!" interrupted Crane. "Later, I'll tell you why."

"Eh bien," resumed Diane, "through error he prematurely took some of those drugs sooner than the *émir* intended. Before the ritual started. And you saw —"

"Plenty." Crane shuddered. Then he glanced at Madeline. "You little fool, you had to follow me!"

"But yes. I suspected that through no fault of your own you had been involved and were following some insane American impulse to do what you thought the right thing. So I followed, to help if I could. I feared she was dead, so I hesitated to call the police."

"Damn lucky you didn't!"

And then Diane interposed, "Monsieur Denis, how can I ever express my gratitude —"

"Madeline," interrupted Crane, "has already taken care of that. And having had my fill of sunny France, I think I'll leave for Spain in the morning." 🦇

E. Hoffman Price, one of the "Lovecraft circle" of writers, remains most famous for his fantasy and horror stories in Weird Tales. *However, he was a frequent and popular contributor to many pulps. This tale originally appeared in the April, 1936 issue of* Spicy Mystery Stories. *Wildside Press released his collection,* Satan's Daughter and Other Tales from the Pulps, *in 2004.*

NOW AVAILABLE . . .

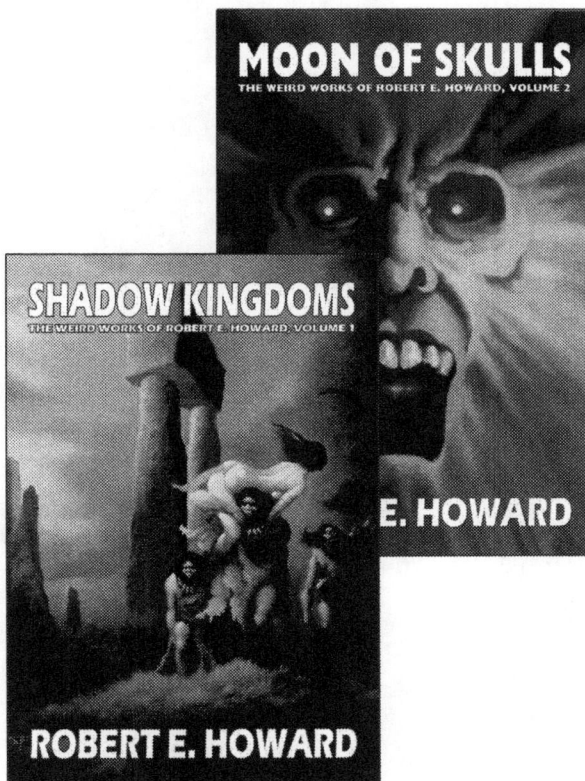

www.ingramcontent.com/pod-product-compliance
Lightning Source LLC
Chambersburg PA
CBHW081156090426
42736CB00017B/3350